Assessing Language through Computer Technology

THE CAMBRIDGE LANGUAGE ASSESSMENT SERIES

Series editors: J. Charles Alderson and Lyle F. Bachman

In this series:

Assessing Language through Computer Technology

Carol A. Chapelle
and
Dan Douglas

CAMBRIDGE
UNIVERSITY PRESS

CAMBRIDGE UNIVERSITY PRESS
Cambridge, New York, Melbourne, Madrid, Cape Town, Singapore, São Paulo

Cambridge University Press
The Edinburgh Building, Cambridge CB2 2RU, UK

www.cambridge.org
Information on this title: www.cambridge.org/9780521549493

First published 2006

Printed in the United Kingdom at the University Press, Cambridge

A catalogue record for this publication is available from the British Library

Library of Congress Cataloging-in-Publication Data

Chapelle, Carol A., 1955-
   Assessing language through computer technology / Carol A. Chapelle and
Dan Douglas.
      p. cm. – (The Cambridge language assessment series)
   Includes bibliographical references and index.
   ISBN-10: 0-521-54949-3 (alk. paper)
   ISBN-10: 0-521-84021-X (alk. paper)
   ISBN-13: 978-0-521-84021-7
   ISBN-13: 978-0-521-54949-3
      1. Language and languages – Ability testing – Data processing.   I. Douglas,
Dan.   II. Title.   III. Series.

   P53.4.C394 2006
   418.00285–dc22   2006002810

For Annie and Webster

Contents

Series editors' preface

Although many people think of computer technology as a recent development, computer technology has been used in language assessment for a long time. Large mainframe computers have been used since the 1960s for the analysis of test data and for the storage of items in databases, or item banks, as well as for producing reports of test results for test users. More recently with the advent of the personal computer, it is now common to use word-processing software for the creation and modification of test tasks, as well as for all of the tasks previously done on a mainframe computer. Perhaps the most striking change that computer and information technology has brought to language assessment, however, is the potential for delivering a wide variety of test tasks online anywhere in the world, and providing immediate feedback, 24 hours a day, seven days a week. This potential for expanding the kinds of tasks that we can deliver to test takers has been accompanied by ever-increasing capacity for scoring responses by computer. While selected-response items have been scored by optical scanners for half a century, recent advances in natural language processing and latent semantic analysis, along with improvements in scanning technology, have made it possible to score written responses to constructed response tasks – both open-ended and short-answer tasks and responses to composition prompts – by computer.

However, along with these potential advances come potential problems and concerns. To what extent might the use of multimedia in assessment tasks introduce features that actually diminish the validity of the interpretations and uses we make of assessment results? For example, how does the use of video in a listening test affect test takers' performance? Does watching a video involve the same abilities as listening to a tape recording? If not, can we interpret scores from audio- and video-delivered tests in the same way? How do we know that scores of written essays produced by human raters can be interpreted in the same way as those produced by computers?

Thus, assessing language through computer technology is not without controversy, and debate is ongoing as to whether the advantages of computer-assisted language testing (CALT) outweigh the disadvantages. Critics argue that CALT constitutes a conservative element in test design, since test items are limited to those types which can be marked by machine. Proponents argue that CALT allows the incorporation of multimedia into tests, that the provision of immediate feedback presents significantly added value to the user, and that as technology develops, even the limitations of computer scoring will diminish as more intelligent scoring algorithms are developed. One frequently proclaimed advantage of CALT is the ability to tailor the test to the individual test taker, in computer-adaptive testing, by selecting the next item to which a test taker is exposed in the light of his or her response to the previous item. Thus if a test taker gets the item wrong, he or she will be presented with an easier item, whereas if the response is correct, the test taker will be presented with a more difficult item. This oft-proclaimed advantage has, however, serious costs associated with it. Firstly, test items need to be trialed on large numbers of test takers to ensure that the items are stable and accurately measure what they are intended to measure. Secondly, for high-stakes tests, very large numbers of pre-tested items are needed to refresh the item banks to ensure test security.

Such is an example of the discussions that surround language assessment through technology, and so this latest addition to the Cambridge Language Assessment Series is very timely. Carol Chapelle and Dan Douglas are experts in the field of language testing in general and in technology-based assessment in particular, having published widely, and having taught courses in these areas at universities and international institutes around the world. In addition, these two authors bring to this volume a wealth of combined knowledge about computer-assisted language learning and second language acquisition research. Furthermore, both have extensive experience in teacher training and in working with practitioners. Their combined experience has been brought to bear on a topic that can only increase in importance and impact. Therefore any person involved in language assessment, at whatever educational level, will need to be familiar with the possibilities and limitations that they should consider when deciding whether to construct or use assessment procedures using computer technology.

The authors present a critical review of research that has sought to address controversial issues, such as whether computer-assisted language tests are equivalent to paper-and-pencil-tests, whether CALT can enhance test validity, what impact CALT might have, and they discuss these issues at length, from both theoretical and practical perspectives. Readers are also given a detailed account of test-authoring software and made aware of the advantages of such systems. Above all, Chapelle and Douglas discuss the ways in which CALT should be evaluated, and how traditional views of test validity need to be both taken into account and adjusted in light of the challenges presented by assessment using technology.

This book will be required reading for any test developer.

J. Charles Alderson
Lyle F. Bachman

Acknowledgments

We would like to extend our sincere thanks to Charles Alderson and Lyle Bachman for their guidance throughout our writing of this last book in the Cambridge Language Assessment Series. The complex topic addressed in this volume is one about which no single person has thorough expertise, and we have therefore benefited greatly from the assistance provided by Charles and Lyle. As authors of the final book in the series, we also take this opportunity to salute their foresight and ambition in proposing such a series and in seeing it through with such rigorous scholarly attention.

Our knowledge and interests in computer technology for assessing language abilities have developed over the past twenty-plus years as we have worked on projects with various people. Most notable of our collaborators are Volker Hegelheimer and Joan Jamieson, both of whom have taken us through ambitious technology projects with their management finesse, technical knowledge, and can-do spirit. Through work with them, we have learned a lot of what is reflected in this volume, which we hope will in turn teach others. We have also benefited through many years of rich interaction with the TOEFL program at Educational Testing Service and with Pearson Education.

We would like to express our appreciation to Mickey Bonin, who was the Cambridge editor in charge of the series when we began this project, and to Jane Walsh, who now oversees the project. We thank Marie Allan, Jacque French, and Clive Rumble for their professional and efficient help with editing and production.

Finally, we express our thanks to the following for permission to reprint their copyrighted material: ACT Inc., Discovery School, Educational Testing Service, Half-baked, IBM Corporation, John Benjamins Publishing, *Journal of Technology, Learning and Assessment*, Ordinate Corporation, Respondus, WebCT, and *Studies in Language Learning*.

CHAPTER ONE

The technology thread

It would be difficult to estimate how many second language learners today have taken or will take a language test delivered by computer, but many high- and low-stakes tests are delivered by computer and the number is rapidly increasing. This fact of language testing in practice is reflected in a thread that runs through the Cambridge Language Assessment Series. The author of each book in the series suggests that computer technology plays a role in language assessment, and particularly in its future. In his survey of vocabulary assessments, for example, Read (2000) includes the computer-based Eurocentres Vocabulary Size Test and the Test of English as a Foreign Language. Beyond this discussion of computer-delivered tests, however, he points out that computer-assisted methodologies are essential for an understanding of vocabulary that is needed to move vocabulary assessment forward. Similarly, Buck (2001) suggests that a critical issue for the future of listening comprehension assessment is presentation of oral language with the support of computer-delivered multimedia. Weigle's (2002) discussion of the future of writing assessment touches upon both the technology-assisted methods of writing assessment, such as computer scoring of written language, and the effects of technology on writing. Alderson (2000) discusses development of a large-scale Web-based test, computer-assisted testing methods for reading, as well as the construct of reading online. Douglas discusses "the pitfalls of technology" (Douglas, 2000, pp. 275ff.) in *Assessing Languages for Specific Purposes*.

Taken together, the strands of the technology thread point to an important change in the fabric of language assessment: the comprehensive introduction of technology. In this volume, we examine the important developments implied by the new uses of technology for language assessment and explore the changes in professional knowledge required by the use of technology. Throughout the book we use the terms "test" and "assessment" interchangeably as we discuss a full range of high-stakes and low-stakes uses of assessments that draw on technology for constructing test tasks and scoring examinee performance. We have not included the many other uses of computers for data handling, and statistical analysis of what we refer to as traditional or non-computer tests (see Davidson 1996 and Bachman 2004, respectively, for discussion of these topics). In related areas of applied linguistics, such as the study of language use, second language acquisition research and second language teaching, technology has had notable impacts on professional knowledge and practice. In all of these areas, research and practice demonstrate that technology expands and changes the conceptual and practical demands placed on those who use it, and that the new demands can often probe users' understanding of their work in applied linguistics.

In language assessment, as well, exploration of technology for testing has increased to the point that today no matter where second language learners live, they will sooner or later take a computer-assisted language test. One of the largest and best-known second language testing programs in the world, the Test of English as a Foreign Language (TOEFL), is delivered by computer in many countries, and several hundred thousand candidates take it annually (Educational Testing Service, TOEFL Program: http://www.ets.org/toefl/). Likewise in many classrooms and language programs online learning materials such as Longman English Interactive (Rost, 2003) incorporate assessments that serve as diagnostic or achievement tests. The mention of computer-assisted assessment in the other books in this series along with the growing number of testing and instructional programs offering online assessment suggest the importance of technology for the future of assessment. In this book, we expand on this suggestion by discussing the differences that computer-assisted language testing (CALT) makes for language assessment. The people most affected by the changes are test takers, of course, because they are the ones who ultimately use the technology. However, the intended readers of this volume are the professionals who work to help the learners and therefore we begin in this chapter by outlining some of the implications of CALT for teachers, test developers, and language-testing researchers.

Language teachers

Language teachers need a solid understanding of assessment because they help learners to develop self-assessment strategies, test learners in the classroom, select or develop tests for language programs and prepare learners to take tests beyond the classroom and language program. Many teachers meet their responsibility for preparing learners to take high-stakes computer-based language tests with some feelings of anxiety and even anger because of the possibility that taking a language test online may disadvantage learners, keeping them from demonstrating the full extent of their ability. Issues of fairness to examinees are only one set of the concerns that technology raises for the testing process. Others include the knowledge required for selection, use and development of computer-assisted tests. At the same time, teachers and learners may benefit by having access to assessment for placements and diagnosis which may or may not be connected to online instruction, and may offer possibilities for response analysis, feedback, and record keeping beyond what is feasible with traditional assessments.

Selection of tests

Teachers are likely to have the opportunity to choose from among a variety of computer-assisted tests and therefore need to have an idea of how such tests can best be evaluated. Do guidelines from educational measurement for analyzing reliability, validity, practicality, and authenticity, for example, cover all the relevant considerations for evaluation of computer-based language assessment? As in the case of the evaluation of computer-assisted language materials (Susser, 2001), evaluation checklists have been proposed for computer-based tests (Noijons, 1994). They include factors that one might find on any test quality checklist (e.g., clear instructions) with modifications pertaining to the technology (e.g., information about help options). Other points, however, are unique to the physical and temporal circumstances of computer-assisted testing (e.g., security of test response data upon test completion). Such checklists have been drawn primarily from educational measurement (e.g., Green, 1988), and therefore they are expected to form a solid foundation but we should also question the extent to which they include all of the concerns relevant to language assessment. For example, tests in other areas very rarely include any spoken language, and therefore the issues concerning speaking and listening through the computer are likely to be under-analyzed in such frameworks. We will discuss the evaluation of CALT in Chapter 5.

Classroom assessment

More and more frequently, teachers have access to computer-assisted language tests that are included as part of online language courses, or to the authoring software that allows teachers to create their own tests. Such classroom assessments raise interesting possibilities for assessing student learning systematically and with provision for detailed feedback. This possibility has been identified as one of the potential attractions of CALT from the early days of the use of technology for language learning (Otto, 1989).

An early example was the French curriculum on the PLATO computer system at the University of Illinois, which kept records on the learners' performance during each session of their work over the course of the semester and provided them with summary information about their performance when they requested it (Marty, 1981). The example Marty provided, called the "General Performance Analysis," could be requested by the learner at any point during the semester. The analysis would tell the student, for example, that he or she had worked on 298 grammar categories, and that overall a score of 77% had been obtained across all categories. Upon request, the learner could obtain a more detailed analysis by asking to see the categories in which he or she had scored below 40%. Figure 1.1 depicts the type of feedback that appeared on the screen in response to such a request. The first column refers to a grammar code, the

1	30%	12	Assez with modifier
21	30%	13	De-verb + partitive
37	20%	19	Verb + de + infinitive
42	10%	14	Ne pas not split with infinitive

Press DATA to enter a different score

Press SHIFT-LAB to review a grammar item

Figure 1.1 Analysis of learners' errors from French learning materials (from Marty, 1981, p. 39).

second is the percentage correct, and the third is the number of items that the learner completed on the particular grammatical point. In addition to the grammar code, the learners were given a description of each grammatical point that they would recognize from instruction.

These diagnostic assessments were built over a period of 20 years in an environment where research and development on French language learning and teaching went hand in hand. The complexity inherent in computer-assisted diagnostic assessment calls for a sustained research agenda rather than a one-time project, as description of the large-scale DIALANG project reveals (Alderson, 2000). Commercial publishers with the resources to develop sophisticated online materials are beginning to draw on some of these ideas about diagnostic assessment or achievements designed to match the courses. Online courses in English, such as Market Leader (Longman, 2002), have an integrated assessment component throughout the courses to give pre- and post-test information to learners and teachers. Such tests are developed through application of the well-known principles of criterion-referenced testing, but the example from the French course illustrates that these basic principles can play out differently for development of online tests.

Whenever language instruction is offered online, it makes sense for teachers to at least consider online assessment as well. However, even some stand-alone tests might best be administered by computer when detailed diagnostic information is desired. For example, years ago, Molholt and Presler (1986) suggested that their pronunciation analysis might be used to identify specific aspects of pronunciation in need of instruction. Canale (1986) advocated looking toward intelligent tutoring systems which would be able to gather diagnostic information about learners as they worked online, and a number of such systems have been described for language learning, but such research has largely emphasized the instructional potential of the systems without fully exploring them as assessments (e.g., Holland, Kaplan & Sams, 1994). Future exploration of the detailed information obtained through diagnostic assessment offers interesting challenges to language assessment as a discipline. As Clark (1989) pointed out, diagnostic tests are developed according to different specifications from those used to construct a proficiency test from which a single score is to be obtained. However, the large part of the theoretical and practical knowledge about developing and interpreting assessments has been cultivated for proficiency-type tests, leaving issues of diagnosis somewhat uncharted territory. As more and more people become interested in and capable of developing and using computer-assisted diagnostic assessments, the issues are likely to be better understood (see Alderson, 2005, for a discussion of these issues).

Test development

Classroom assessments are frequently developed by teachers themselves so as to reflect the important points that were taught in class. Accordingly, a range of options exists for teachers wishing to develop their own online tests. The most efficient option for doing so is course management software that allows the teacher to construct units containing quizzes, that is, to construct the specific questions to be delivered on the quiz and a means for scoring and reporting scores to students and to teachers. Such authoring software is very useful in allowing teachers access to the authoring process with very little training. However, as Chapter 4 will explain, efficiency is often obtained at the expense of the specific features that would be desirable such as a variety of item types and linguistically sensitive response analysis. Nevertheless, such general-purpose authoring software provides teachers access to the authoring process and to some of the capabilities of CALT.

As a consequence, teachers can work together to develop assessments that fit into their program. For example, the English Language Institute (ELI) at the University of Surrey, in the UK, has developed a number of self-access activities designed to complement the courses they offer. The activities include short quizzes which provide instant feedback to learners so they can assess their own learning, as illustrated in Figure 1.2, from a quiz on thesis writing. Teachers and students might benefit from developing and using such an online quiz, which would not require sophisticated authoring tools.

Test developers

Professional developers of computer-assisted tests work with a much wider set of options than that which used to be available for test development including delivery options that expand the ways in which language can be assessed. New methods include computer-adaptive testing, the use of multimedia for presenting linguistic and visual input for learners, and automatic response analysis. These new methods raise questions for test developers about what the new language tests are measuring.

Thesis1
Thank you for taking the Thesis Writing Unit 1 Self-Access Quiz

---

· 1

- 3 out of 5

Section 1: Preparation In the preparation stage of your thesis, before you actually embark upon your research, once you have decided your topic, a number of activities are of particular importance. In the following list, select the 5 most important activities.

✔

Establishing objectives was correct
A correct answer was Writing initial outline proposals

Formulating the title helps clarify your thinking at the beginning, even if you change your mind later. You need to establish objectives as soon as possible, to make sure that your research has a clear direction. This also makes it easier to select reading! Initial outline proposals also help to clarify issues. The focus of the topic is crucial: it must not be too broad or too narrow. Finally, it is always important to write a timetable to establish deadlines for completing work.

Figure 1.2   Surrey ELI Self-Access Quiz feedback
          (http://www.surrey.ac.uk/ELI/sa/thesis1.html).

Computer-adaptive testing

Many professional test developers associate computers for test delivery with the development of large pools of items for computer-adaptive tests (CATs). A computer-adaptive test selects and presents items in a sequence based on the test taker's response to each item. If an examinee gets the first question correct, a more difficult question is selected from a pool and presented next; if this one is answered correctly, a more difficult one is selected. If the candidate misses a question, the algorithm selects an easier one for the next question, and so on. A CAT program "learns" about the examinee's level by monitoring the difficulty of the items the test taker gets right and wrong and thus begins to select only those items at the candidate's level of ability. When the program has presented enough items to be able to estimate the test taker's ability at a predetermined level of reliability, the test ends and a score can be reported. CATs are efficient because they present items to test takers close to their level of ability, thus avoiding items that are either too easy or too difficult and which consequently would not offer much information about a test taker's abilities.

Test developers were introduced to the advantages of computer-adaptive testing at least 20 years ago. Tung (1986) outlined the following advantages: they require fewer items than their paper counterparts, they avoid challenging examinees far beyond their capability by selecting items at the appropriate difficulty level, and they offer improved security by selecting from an item pool to construct individualized tests. CATs became possible through developments in measurement theory called Item Response Theory (Lord, 1980; Hambleton, Swaminathan & Rogers, 1991), a means for obtaining robust statistical data on test items, and through advances in computer software for calculating the item statistics and providing adaptive control of item selection, presentation and evaluation (Green, Bock, Humphreys, Linn & Reckase, 1984; Wainer, Dorans, Flaugher, Green, Mislevy, Steinberg & Thissen, 1990; Brown, 1997). See Bachman (2004, Chapter 3) for an accessible conceptual introduction to IRT.

Following examples in the early 1980s at Brigham Young University developed by Larson and Madsen (1985), other computer adaptive language tests were reported throughout the 1990s (e.g., Kaya-Carton, Carton & Dandonoli, 1991; Burston & Monville-Burston, 1995; Brown & Iwashita, 1996; Young, Shermis, Brutten & Perkins, 1996). Through these projects, important issues were raised about the way language was being measured, about the need for independent items, and about their selection through an adaptive algorithm. In an edited volume in 1999, Chalhoub-Deville brought together a range of theoretical and practical perspectives to discuss computer-adaptive testing for L2 reading. Theoretical papers emphasized the multidimensionality of the reading construct, whereas descriptions of testing practice spoke to the need for unidimensional scores, particularly for placement (e.g., Dunkel, 1999; Laurier, 1999). Results from this work suggest that computer-adaptivity can be used to construct efficient language tests to test language abilities such as reading comprehension, but at the same time most would agree that such tests fail to take advantage of the range of capabilities that the computer offers.

The notion of adaptivity continues to be explored and expanded, and now can refer to any form of branching, or alternative path options, that are chosen for students to take within a program based on their responses. For example, tests of the future might expand on a current example, Longman English Assessment, which branches to either general-purpose or specific business content, depending on the examinee's response to an interest questionnaire at the beginning of the test. In this case, the content of the language of the input is adapted to students' interests, to some extent. In other cases, test tasks might be adapted based on the examinee's level of performance on preceding sections of the test. In short, test developers have barely begun to scratch the surface of the ways in which a test might be tailored to fit the examinee. This is an area in which technology challenges test developers to construct tests that are suited to the needs and interests of learners.

Multimedia tasks

Another potentially powerful option that computers offer test developers is the provision for rich multimodal input in the form of full motion video, text, sound, and color graphics, potentially enhancing authenticity of both input and response. Test developers are concerned with enhancement of two aspects for authenticity: *situational authenticity*, which defines authenticity in terms of the features of context including setting, participants, content, tone, and genre, and *interactional authenticity*, which defines authenticity in terms of the interaction, between the test taker's language knowledge and the communicative task (Bachman 1991). In some cases, multimedia can help to portray these aspects of a non-test situation on a test. For example, a placement test, in the Web-based Language Assessment System (WebLAS), at the University of California, Los Angeles, developed to provide information about placement, progress, diagnosis, and achievement in second and foreign language teaching programs at UCLA, uses video to present lecture content for comprehension tasks. The use of the video is intended to enhance the situational authenticity of the test by depicting the features of academic context such as a classroom, white board, and PowerPoint slides. One can envisage other situations such as following a tour guide, checking in at a hotel, or participating in a business meeting where the video would also add to the non-test context that the test is intended to portray. Examples of such scenarios are contained in multimedia software for language learning, which provide good examples of possibilities for test developers.

Automatic response analysis

Tests which call on the examinee to produce language hold the potential for increasing interactional authenticity over those that require selected responses since the former typically require a greater breadth and depth of language knowledge and background knowledge, and more sophisticated use of strategic competence. Some language test developers have explored the use of natural language processing technologies to construct scoring procedures for examinees' linguistic production. An automated speaking assessment, PhonePass (Ordinate Corporation, 2002b), for example, scores the accuracy of repeated words, pronunciation, reading fluency, and repeat fluency, based on a computer speech recognition system containing an algorithm derived from a large spoken corpus of native speakers of various English regional and social dialects. The Educational Testing Service, which produces the TOEFL as well as a number of other academic and professional tests, has developed an automated system, Criterion (2005a), for rating extended written responses, based on natural language processing (NLP) technology that syntactically parses input, identifies discourse structural information of selected units of text, and analyzes topical vocabulary, to produce a holistic rating of an essay on a six-point scale.

New test methods, new constructs?

In the first collection of papers on CALT, Canale (1986) pointed out that the use of the computer held the promise of providing a better means for measuring different language constructs than that which was possible with traditional test methods. However, research and development has tended to focus on the goals of increasing efficiency and authenticity of testing, whereas to date few researchers have explored the intriguing questions of how the computer might be used to assess different abilities, or constructs, than those currently assessed by traditional methods. These issues were discussed by Alderson, who outlined computer capabilities relevant to exploring an innovative agenda for CALT:

1. The computer has the ability to measure time. The time which a learner takes to complete a task, or even the time taken on different parts of a task, can be measured, controlled and recorded by computer.
2. The computer has the ability to record information about the testee's routes through the test.
3. The computer can present information in a variety of ways.
4. The computer can provide quick and easy access to a variety of different types of information.
5. The computer can be linked to other equipment. This can allow different types of input and presentation.
6. The computer can encourage the learner's own strategies for evaluation. In particular the information which a computer can collate and present about test performance could help the learner to feel that his own opinions are of importance.
7. The computer can make use of language rules. a. At a relatively simple level the computer can do a spelling check on the learner's text. b. Parsers of varying degrees of sophistication can be used not only to check for syntactic errors in the learner's text, but to provide "communicative" tests as well.

(Alderson, 1990, pp. 39–43)

At about the same time that Alderson was exploring CALT-related issues and possibilities in England, Corbel was working on the same problem in Australia. Corbel (1993) enumerated the potentials in need of further exploration as questions that might serve as a starting point for a research agenda:

1. Can the need for variations in tests be catered for by the use of computer-based simulations that branch according to aspects of context and purpose?
2. Can the concept of communicative task-based tests be operationalized more adequately by computer?
3. Can the use of comment banks and profiles provide some way of reflecting the multidimensionality of language proficiency? Can information of diagnostic value be captured? Is it usable and relevant to internal and external audiences? How reliable are the components of profiles?
4. Can computers enhance the training and moderation of raters using proficiency scales?
5. What forms of support are needed for the participants — teachers and learners? Can the support be computer-based?
6. Can the computer enhance the process of the learner's self-assessment?

7. Can the computer provide the means to present innovative testing techniques while retaining reliability and validity?

8. How can the data gathered through computer-assisted tests inform related areas?

9. What can computer test developers learn from "intelligent" computer applications?   (Corbel, 1993, p. 53)

A look at the current work in language assessment reveals some exploration of the ideas Alderson and Corbel suggested but these significant issues have not been explored extensively or systematically. Doing so falls within the domain of language-testing researchers who typically take the first steps in understanding how new testing methods can change and improve the constructs measured by CALT.

Language testing researchers

Beyond the issues of concern to teachers and test developers, language testing researchers might be offered new opportunities for theorizing and researching language tests through the use of technology. To give an indication of how the use of technology amplifies and probes important research questions, Chapelle (2003) outlined areas of concern to researchers, three of which focus on better understanding test constructs and two of which probe validation issues.

Clarifying test constructs

Theoretical questions about test constructs are probed when test designers are faced with decisions about the extent to which individual examinees are given choices during test taking such as whether or not they should be allowed to return to a listening passage more than once. If a test offers examinees options such as repeated listening, help with word definitions, or a clock, the examinee's score will reflect not only listening ability, but also his or her strategic use of these options. These issues of test design require the researcher to consider the strategic competence to be included in the construct definition underlying the test, and therefore to reconsider the issue of construct definition. For example, the computer-based TOEFL provides a help option in the lower right corner of the screen that test takers may go to during the test for information on how to respond to a particular item format, as illustrated in Figure 1.3.

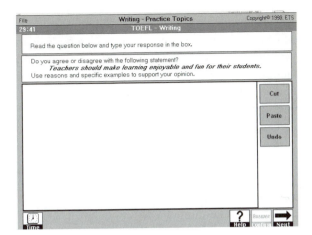

Figure 1.3 Screen from TOEFL sample test
(Educational Testing Service, 1999).

The "Help" button at the lower right, and the timer at the upper left, which may be turned off with the button at the lower left, offer options that each test taker him- or herself must decide how to use. It is not clear how test takers' availing themselves of these options might affect their performance and thus the interpretation of their language abilities. For example, test takers may click on the help button at any time during their writing to get help on how to manipulate the relevant keys such as *backspace, delete, home, end, arrows, page up, page down,* and *enter.* Time spent receiving help is subtracted from actual writing time, and therefore the efficient use of these options is essential. The resulting test score must be interpreted to mean both writing ability and strategic competence for effective use of online help.

An analogous issue is evident in the measurement of listening comprehension. Language-testing researchers are wrestling with questions such as whether a theoretical definition of listening comprehension should assume that input includes visual cues (Gruba, 1997) and how authenticity can best be developed in view of a complex set of options. For example, Coniam (2001) argues for the authenticity of a listening test with video on the one hand based on the assumption that examinees' "contact with and exposure to English language in Hong Kong is more likely to be from television ... than from radio" (p. 3). On the other hand, he ultimately decided that, "a listening test needs to be primarily concerned with assessing listening," and the video threatens this objective. He argues, "While the test's perceived authenticity may be enhanced, the test's validity may be compromised" (Coniam, 2001, p. 12). It should be evident to language testing researchers that this conclusion might be expressed more precisely as an important issue about the definition of the listening construct that the test is intended to measure and the domain to which test users need to be able to extrapolate score meaning. Moreover, it was the availability of the video for test development that opened the important issue about the construct.

Detailing test constructs

A second issue that probes construct definition in novel ways is the scoring of examinees' responses through computer-assisted scoring algorithms. When a computer program is developed to analyze and score learners' language, the test developer has to make precise decisions about what is more and less correct of the many possible responses that might be given. Such decisions need to be based on the construct to be measured, but construct theory expressed in general terms such as "writing ability" or "vocabulary knowledge" does not provide sufficient guidance for making such specific decisions about scoring. CALT, therefore, presses the researcher to consider how to develop more detailed construct theory.

This issue is evident in the discomfort many language-testing researchers feel at the thought of Criterion, mentioned earlier in this chapter. Based on NLP technology, Criterion parses textual input, assigning grammatical labels to constituents in the examinee's response and identifying markers of discourse structure and content vocabulary. The score Criterion assigns is derived from the NLP analysis: the lexical analysis signals the extent to which the examinee has addressed the task and the complexity of the response, the discourse analysis rates the organization and development, and the parser's analysis results in a rating of syntactic quality. In other words, the construct, or meaning, of "writing ability" as defined by Criterion is derived from features of the essay that the computer is able to recognize: content vocabulary, discourse markers, and certain syntactic categories (Educational Testing Service, 2005a). Researchers advocating a richer, more complex definition of writing ability may criticize Criterion as operationalizing the construct of writing ability in a way that is driven by the available technology, but one might also note that the technology provides an impetus for specifying precisely how writing is operationalized.

To date, the few investigations of computer-assisted response analysis reported have been exploratory (Chapelle, 1993; Holland, 1994; Coniam, 1998; Carr, Pan & Xi, 2002), raising more questions than they answer. However, even the small amount of work in this complex area points to critical questions that probe issues of construct definition. First, when responses are scored on the basis of computational analysis, researchers are prompted to develop principles for scoring rather than making a yes/no decision as to whether the examinee's response matched the key. Even single-word responses in a cloze test represent data that might be analyzed in many different ways depending on what the test is intended to measure. For example, a scoring program that records performance data might identify and record correct and incorrect production of spelling, semantic and syntactic fit, derivational suffixes, and inflectional morphemes (Chapelle, 2003, Chapter 6). Each of these five aspects of a single-word response might be more or less accurate relative to the sentence and text context. Therefore, for a single-word response, an analysis program might evaluate at least three levels of correctness for five components, so the total score variation for a single word would be 15 points. This potential 15-point variation should be derived in a way that is consistent with the intended construct meaning of the test. Second, if such scoring procedures result in component scores (e.g., a score for spelling, another for semantic accuracy) acceptable ways are needed for estimating the reliability of component scores in a way that is consistent with the construct definition. Such methods have been explored (e.g., Embretson, 1985; Ackerman, 1994), but they have not been applied in a theoretically motivated way to examine language-testing data in view of a detailed construct definition.

Rethinking validation

Validation issues also stem from the researcher's perspective on the need to better understand what aspects of language ability can be measured using a computer. The issues arise when a researcher approaches validation using only correlational methods to investigate the relationship between tests delivered online and those delivered without technology. This paradigm assumes that all language tests should measure language traits that are realized in the same way across different contexts of language use. The assumption underlying this validation method has been challenged by theory related to assessment of language for specific purposes (LSP). If the test of English listening for agriculture, for example, is expected to correlate strongly with the test of English listening for computer science, the whole concept of specific purpose competence is undermined. Based on the idea that the abilities across different registers of language use should be expected to be different, Douglas (1998) pointed out that factors (e.g., "method effects") other than a language trait should not necessarily be considered sources of error:

> Rather than attempting to minimize method effects, ...we need to capitalize on them by designing tests for specific populations — tests that contain instructions, content, genre, and language directed toward that population.   (Douglas, 1998, p. 153).

If an English test for prospective students at colleges and universities requires examinees to manipulate a mouse to select responses in a listening test, for example, the question, according to Douglas, should be whether or not that method assesses relevant or irrelevant abilities, not whether or not it strengthens or weakens a correlation with another test. LSP testing offers clear cases for the issue of what should be included in language constructs, whereas technology presents a more subtle, and even insidious, case. The computer is the vehicle of delivery for language tests that may be intended to measure general traits (e.g., grammar, reading comprehension) and it may exert specific effects on the language being tested. At the same time, technology is actually changing the way language is used and therefore the abilities required to use it (e.g., Crystal, 2001). The complexity of validation issues for computer-assisted language assessment defies a simplistic or prescriptive approach to validation. Instead researchers are challenged to examine and question previously held assumptions and to develop defensible alternatives.

Connecting to Second Language acquisition (SLA) research

As Alderson and Corbel hinted in their exploration of possibilities for the computer, technology allows for different constructs to be measured, particularly, for example, those assessed through time keeping. In SLA research, the amount of time delay before a learner responds to a question has been interpreted as an indicator of automaticity in a research task (Hagen, 1994) or as advance preparation in an instructional task

(Jamieson & Chapelle, 1987). In such studies computer-assisted assessment offers a means of measuring constructs of interest for the study of language acquisition and use that are not available through performance on paper-and-pencil tests. Moreover, such processes can be assessed during the course of participation in normal online learning activities, raising the possibility of online diagnostic assessment of some strategies. At the same time, since such assessments are different from the familiar grammaticality judgments, self-reports, etc. used in SLA research, they raise important questions about the validity of inferences in SLA research tasks. For example, Hegelheimer and Chapelle (2000) suggest that mouse clicks used to request definitions for vocabulary might be used as an indicator of noticing, which is a construct of interest in SLA research, but that at the same time such an inference raises questions about accepted methods for justifying inferences.

Investigating test consequences

Since early in the introduction of technology into language assessment, researchers have been interested in whether or not test takers' apprehension about computer use might affect their language performance. The question was whether negative effects could be documented and if so how they could be minimized. With the passing of time, the question is rapidly losing its importance because test takers are becoming more and more comfortable with computer technology. In fact, today we have students who express anxiety about the prospect of writing a final exam *without* a computer. In the meantime, on the other hand, we know very little about how computer anxiety affects test takers. At present, test developers provide support for test takers who may not yet feel at ease with the technology. Perhaps the best-known example is the tutorial that precedes the computer-based TOEFL (Jamieson, Kirsch, Taylor & Eignor, 1999). The idea of the tutorial is to give all learners an opportunity to familiarize themselves with the editing and control functions of the computer before beginning the test in order to dramatically diminish the possibility that variance in test performance would be in part attributable to variance in computer familiarity.

Technology underscores the need for researchers to investigate consequences of testing in a way that reveals the effects of computer-delivered tests, as some researchers have done for paper-and-pencil tests (e.g., Alderson & Hamp-Lyons, 1996). However, an equally important perspective on consequences is the proactive development of testing practices that may benefit examinees by urging them and their teachers to begin working with and learning through technology. In other words, CALT may hold the potential for a type of positive washback if one considers the benefits that many believe are associated with regular access to technology during second language learning. Many teachers and researchers argue that students should have access to learning materials online in the hope that such practice will increase computer literacy and literacy in the target language. Warschauer (1998), for example, argues that both literacies are critical for success, and therefore important questions for research include "how computer-mediated language and literacy practices are shaped by broader institutional and social factors, as well as what these new practices mean from the perspective of the learner" (Warschauer, 1998, p. 760). The study of consequences of computer-assisted practices in testing might also consider such questions. Validation theory prompts researchers in the future not only to document negative consequences of CALT but also to envisage and investigate potential positive consequences of CALT.

Prospects for CALT

In view of the complex opportunities and challenges technology appears to offer for language assessment, it may be reassuring that some researchers have been studying the implementation and effects of technology in language assessment for over twenty years. Technology was the focus of the 1985 Language Testing Research Colloquium, selected papers from which were published in a volume edited by Stansfield (1986). That volume, which appeared when only a small minority of language testers were working extensively with technology, forecasted many of the issues that would preoccupy language testing research and development over at least the next decade. Some papers in that volume hinted at the complex concerns of the language teacher, test developer and researcher outlined above, but these concerns have not been researched comprehensively or resolved. In this chapter we have argued that the technology thread that was initiated in the 1985 conference and that runs throughout the books in the Cambridge Language Assessment Series is worthy of consideration as a topic on its own. It is a topic that offers new potentials for language test users, including teachers, researchers, and learners.

The following chapter examines the ways in which testing methods implemented through technology are different from those used in the past, which relied on paper and pencil, audio, and face-to-face oral interviews. The differences form a basis for considering the issues of concern to teachers, test developers and researchers, one of which is the question of whether or not such methods can contribute positively to the validity of inferences and uses of assessments. Chapter 3 will discuss the possibility that assessment of language through CALT may distort or change the language abilities measured by the test to the extent that test performance cannot be considered an accurate indication of language ability. This threat of technology will be discussed through consideration of the theoretical and empirical evidence pertaining to the meaning of examinee performance on CALT.

Chapter 4 describes the software tools used for developing CALT and explains concerns for test development through technology that are different than those for other forms of assessments. It discusses options available to developers and describes software concepts in view of their use in language testing. Chapter 5 considers how CALT should best be evaluated: since CALT encompasses notable differences from paper-and-pencil testing, should it be evaluated against a different set of standards than other tests? Chapter 6 discusses the extent to which the changes in testing afforded by technology constitute the type of revolution in testing that some have predicted. We argue that the changes are more evolutionary than revolutionary at this point, and that revolutionary changes will need to be prompted and supported by advances in our understanding of language use and second language acquisition.

Overall, the volume aims to highlight the new potentials offered by technology for language assessment and the issues that these potentials raise. It therefore focuses primarily on how Web-based delivery, interactive technologies, and NLP change the test-taking experience for examinees, test use for teachers, and assessment issues for language test developers and researchers. These are the areas that have received relatively little attention compared to computer-adaptive testing and statistical analysis of numeric test data, both of which are important developments in language assessment made possible by technology.

CHAPTER TWO

What is the CALT difference?

In the previous chapter we argued that teachers, test developers and language-testing researchers need to add to their professional knowledge by learning about how technology is changing the possibilities and realities for language assessment. What are the specific changes implicated by the use of technology in language assessment? We have discussed how technology presents changes that are relevant to the language teacher, language test developer, and language-testing researcher, but in this chapter we will focus specifically on how technology-assisted assessment methods differ from methods available to test developers in the past through paper and pencil, audio/video, and face-to-face oral interviews. We focus on the positive aspects of computer-assisted techniques, and only touch upon some of the problems associated with technology in assessment, a topic we take up more fully in Chapter 3. Our analysis draws on the perspective language-testing researchers have found productive for studying language test methods. From this perspective, it is more informative to consider test methods in terms of specific characteristics that comprise the testing event rather than holistically with terms such as "multiple-choice" or "oral interview" (Bachman, 1990). We begin with a brief discussion of the test method characteristics, and then look at the ways that technology affects each one.

Test method characteristics

Language use is affected by the context in which it takes place. It seems almost too obvious to point out that we use language differently depending upon where we are, whom we are addressing, why we are communicating, what we are communicating about, how we feel about it, and whether we are speaking or writing. However, these differences in language use need to be examined more carefully when a language test is the context of language use. The language use displayed by an examinee during test performance is influenced by the contextual characteristics associated with the task at hand, with the important proviso that a test is a carefully managed, and in a special way, artificial language use situation. It is carefully managed to attempt to treat all test takers fairly and consistently as they work their way through the test; it is artificial in the sense that a test is contrived to reflect as faithfully as possible features of actual language use so that the test performance can be interpreted as evidence of how the test taker might perform in real life. As Carroll defined it nearly 40 years ago, a test is "a procedure designed to elicit certain behavior from which one can make inferences about certain [examinee] characteristics" (Carroll, 1968, p. 46). Today we might modify the last phrase to read "about certain examinee characteristics in particular non-test contexts."

Today language-testing researchers describe test methods in much the same way: the method by which we present the test, the various tasks we ask the test takers to engage in, the ways in which we ask them to respond, and the procedures we use to judge their performances. These characteristics inevitably affect examinees' language use and therefore the measurement of their language ability. Since technology offers new configurations of test methods, it is likely to have an important influence on test takers' language performance. Therefore, it is important to understand how computers are likely to be different from other means of presenting language test tasks and thus how technology may affect interpretations of language test performance. The so-called "method effect" associated with the procedures by which the test is delivered, the responses processed, and the scores derived can reflect both positive and negative effects on the test performance. Positive effects ensue when the test methods mirror characteristics of the target language use situation and/or the aspects of language use the test is intended to measure. Also, positive effects may result when the computer is better able to record or analyze examinees' responses than human raters could. When the test methods diverge significantly from real-world language use or interfere with the measurement of the desired language abilities, the method effect is a negative factor. In either case, it is important for test developers and researchers to be cognizant of, and control to the extent possible, any effects of using computer technology to assist in the measurement of language ability. As have other authors in this series (e.g., Alderson, 2000; Buck, 2001; and Douglas, 2000), we discuss test method differences using a test method framework including the physical and temporal circumstances of the test, the test rubric, input, the expected response, the interaction between input and response, and the characteristics of assessment. This framework has been adapted from those developed by Bachman (1990) and Bachman & Palmer (1996) and Douglas (2000), and is outlined in Table 2.1. Table 2.1 also forecasts the discussion of the advantages and limitations of CALT with respect to each of the characteristics of test method.

The *physical and temporal test circumstances* include the place where the test is taken, the personnel responsible for administering the test, and the time that the test is taken. Bachman and Palmer (1996) use the term *setting* for this characteristic, but we have used the phrase *physical and temporal test circumstances* to distinguish it from the term *setting* as it is used in our discussion of input and response characteristics below. Computer-assisted language tests, particularly if accessible on the Internet, can be convenient for test takers, who can in principle take the test wherever and whenever they can log on. This convenience is limited, though, by security concerns, particularly that of authentication of test taker identity in Web-based test delivery – and the higher the stakes for test takers and score users, the greater the concern – and by the fact that, at least for the near future, standardization of equipment and software, and the expertise required for installation and maintenance will restrict the wherever–whenever ideal in practice. *Rubric* refers to the information given to the test taker about how to proceed with taking the test: instructions, time allocation, test organization, and how to respond to the test tasks. Computers offer the advantage of consistency in presentation of instructions, timing, and parts of the test. In addition, computers allow for a number of innovations such as help screens that test takers can access at will, thus adding an element of discretion. Whereas the former is likely to enhance consistency, the latter may increase variability, thereby affecting measurement of the desired ability.

Test *input* is the material that the test taker is presented with and is expected to comprehend and respond to in some way in carrying out the test tasks. Input might include a prompt, in the case of setting up an essay or role-playing task, for example, and some visual and/or aural information such as a reading text, a chart or picture, or a video clip, which the test takers must process and draw upon their comprehension of in responding

Table 2.1 *Test method characteristics and CALT advantages and limitations*

Test method characteristics	CALT advantages	CALT limitations
Physical and temporal circumstances Location, time, personnel	CALTs can be taken at many convenient locations, at convenient times, and largely without human intervention.	Security is an issue in high-stakes tests; equipment not standardized nor universally available; IT expertise required for establishment, maintenance.
Rubric/Instructions Procedures for responding	Test tasks are presented in a consistent manner for all test takers and instructions and input are presented automatically and uniformly, making for enhanced fairness.	Different levels of instructions, voluntary help screens, different languages of instructions can detract from uniformity.
Input and expected response Features of the context: *setting, participants, tone* Format: *visual/audio/video*	Multimedia capabilities allow for a variety of input and response types, enhancing contextualization and authenticity.	Input and response types are limited by available technology.
Interaction between the Input and Response Reactivity: *reciprocal*	Computers can adapt input in response to test takers' responses and actions, allowing for computer-adaptive tests and rapid feedback.	Interactiveness is more controlled than certain other formats; computer's ability to sample fairly may be limited; CATs are expensive to develop.
Characteristics of assessment Construct definition Criteria for correctness Scoring procedures	Natural language processing (NLP) technology allows for automated scoring of complex responses, affecting the construct definition, scoring criteria, and procedures.	NLP technology is new, expensive, and limited, thus creating potential problems for construct definition and validity.

to questions or performing tasks. The computer technology that affects the delivery of the input also has an effect on the way test takers respond: written responses are typically keyed or clicked in, although handwriting and speaking are increasingly used as well. The use of technology for inputting examinees' responses can be advantageous to the extent that it mirrors how test takers are accustomed to engaging with language in target settings, or problematic in cases where it does not allow them to use response modes that are natural for them. Of course, what learners are accustomed to depends on each individual's instructional and language use background.

The main aspect of the *interaction between the input and response* that will concern us with regard to computer-assisted language testing is the computer's ability to change subsequent input in light of each of the test taker's responses – most commonly in *computer-adaptive tests* (CATs). (See discussion of CATs in Chapter 1, pp. 7–9 above.) The reciprocal interaction that occurs in CATs is qualitatively different from that in conversations among humans. Therefore, the adaptivity afforded by the computer opens new options for interactivity that may serve for tailoring tests to individuals.

Finally, the *characteristics of assessment* refer to the definition of what is to be measured by the test, the criteria by which the performance will be evaluated in terms of that definition, and the process by which the performance will be scored or rated. Computers can assist with scoring in increasingly complex ways, through NLP technology that can emulate some aspects of human judgment. However, NLP is still in its infancy, relatively expensive, and limited in what aspects of spoken and written language it can measure. Therefore, research is needed to investigate the best uses of existing capabilities for response analysis.

The test method characteristics provide an organizing framework for analysis of the CALT difference because they reflect the points of decision making at which test developers affect *what* the test measures by deciding *how* the test measures. Little research revealing the effects of technology choices is available at this point. Therefore, this chapter intends to make explicit the critical points of intersection between technology and test method facets through description, and then the following chapter considers some points of tension at which criticisms have been raised about the use of technology in language testing.

Physical and temporal circumstances

Problems of access for test takers and administrative convenience and expense have long been associated with language testing. Administration conditions of most traditional tests require that test takers present themselves at a designated time and place. For large-scale testing programs, such as the International English Language Testing System (IELTS) and the Michigan English Language Assessment Battery (MELAB), or national examinations, such as the National College English Test in China, test materials must be shipped to testing sites, test takers must travel sometimes great distances to take the test, their responses shipped back to scoring centers, and the results then sent out to test takers and score users. Even for relatively small-scale assessments, such as placement tests or classroom achievement tests, test takers must appear at a designated time and place, where the test administrator or instructor hands out test papers, reads instructions out loud, manipulates equipment such as audiotape players, monitors test procedures and time, collects answer sheets and test materials, and dismisses the test takers. Administering virtually all language tests requires a significant commitment of time and energy.

Computer-assisted tests offer the possibility of diminishing the administrative burden of invigilating, or proctoring, by making the test available wherever and whenever the test taker can log onto the Internet or can insert a disk into a CD-ROM drive. Similarly, computer-assisted tests can reduce administrative burdens by transmitting test materials electronically, and requiring fewer personnel to hand out test papers, collect answer sheets, operate equipment, and so on. The use of the Internet for test delivery is of particular interest to test developers wishing to capitalize on technology for improving access. Increased access is perhaps the most noted benefit cited by enthusiasts of Web-based testing such as Roever (2001):

> Probably the single biggest logistical advantage of a WBT [Web-based Test] is its flexibility in time and space. All that is required to take a WBT is a computer with a Web browser and an Internet connection (or the test on disk). Test takers can take the WBT whenever and wherever it is convenient, and test designers can share their test with colleagues all over the world and receive feedback. (p. 88)

An example of a Web-based test intended to provide convenient access to a broad range of users was developed to offer a means for European citizens to have their skills and knowledge assessed and recognized outside formal qualification systems (DIALANG, 2001). Users are able to choose their preferred language for test instructions and feedback, and they can also choose in which language and skill areas (reading, writing, listening, grammatical structures, vocabulary) they want to be tested. DIALANG realizes the main promises of CALT for test takers and administrators through the convenience of Web-based access and delivery. Users can access this low-stakes test at their own convenience whenever and wherever they can log onto the Web. DIALANG even provides for test takers to self-rate their own writing, using a set of benchmarks (Luoma and Tarnanen 2003). From the test administrator's point of view, the test is entirely self-managed, and administration consists primarily of data collection and troubleshooting. When the test is fully operational, it may be possible for administrators to collect data on item performance; the amount of time users take for each item, subtests, and the entire test; self-assessment; test–retest; and self-reported demographics on the users. Routine collection of these data would make constant revision a possibility. These anticipated options intend to take advantage of the Web-based benefits in a low-stakes test setting, but such options as self-access and self-rating would obviously have to be handled differently for high-stakes testing.

Rubric and instructions

A perennial concern for traditional language testing is the variation that occurs from one administration to another in how instructions are presented and in how timing of each section is controlled and monitored. Instructions may be read, or sometimes presented extemporaneously, by administrators in large examination rooms where acoustics may vary greatly for examinees sitting in different locations. The actual content of the instructions may differ depending on the experience and frame of mind of the administrator. Time keeping for each section or task can be another source of variation from one administration to the next. By contrast, computer-based test instructions are presented in a consistent manner for all test takers, and timing of tasks and sections is automatic and reliable. At the same time, computers offer flexibility in how and when instructions are delivered and in what language. For example, the Business Language Testing Service (BULATS), permits the test taker to receive the instructions in one of six European languages.

Another aspect of the rubric and instructions in language testing is the provision of test preparation and practice materials. Such materials for most non-computer tests are usually completely separate from the "live" test and although they may be similar in format and test-taking conditions to the actual test, they may also vary to some extent. An important difference in CALT is the easy, widespread availability of test preparation and practice materials that can be taken under conditions very similar to those in the "live" test. Materials published online or on CD-ROM give test takers practice with the task formats and procedures for responding that they will encounter in the actual test. For example, the TOEFL website (http://www.ets.org/toefl) offers a number of options for obtaining preparation materials, including a free online practice test.

Consistency and uniformity in the rubric and instructions and the ease of access to preparation materials represent an important difference for CALT. Since all test takers receive precisely the same input no matter where or when they take the test, and since test takers have access to tutorial and practice materials in the same medium as the test itself, test takers should feel that they have a fair opportunity to succeed. At the same time, the complexity of the delivery systems and test-taking procedures for CALT may create the need for tutorials and practice material that is greater for CALT than for other test formats.

Input and expected response

Computers can be used to display and process large amounts of data rapidly allowing for the input the examinee receives on a language test to include rich contextual information consisting of images, sounds, and full-motion video, potentially enhancing authenticity in both the input and response. This capability opens the possibility for addressing a consistent problem in language testing: that tests are usually seen as consisting of input and tasks that are too decontextualized relative to the language use of interest to test users. This is a problem affecting authenticity because real-life language use is embedded in social and psychological contexts, whereas many traditional tests contain contrived language that must be somehow recontextualized. The question is how this contextualization can be most effectively carried out. Although non-CALT tests have employed some effective contextualization techniques, they are generally limited to what can be accomplished by means of print combined with audio/video mediums, and to live interviews and role-plays which are subject to the creativity, indeed the acting ability, of the interviewers. Presenting test tasks that reflect the variety and complexity of language in communicative use is thus a constant challenge for language test developers.

CALT offers test developers new options for presenting input material in a variety of media, including text, graphics, audio, and video, as well as in user control of the input. To the extent that multimodal input reflects characteristics of the target language use situation, it has the potential to enhance authenticity as well as increase the intrinsic interest of the test tasks themselves, strengthening the possibility for greater interaction between the test taker's communicative language ability and the test tasks. In Chapter 1 we discussed an example from the UCLA WebLAS test, in which the listening component in the sample test contains a video text of approximately six-and-a-half minutes from a psychology lecture on the topic of memory retrieval (UCLA, 2001). Test takers see a small-screen video of a lecturer speaking and using an overhead projector to write outline notes on a screen, moving around, gesturing, using facial expression, and so on. Such a format would be seen by most test developers as attaining high authenticity relative to the context of a classroom lecture because the test taker can see elements of a classroom setting, including the projector and screen and a blackboard in the background, hear the lecturer presenting a moderately formal academic lecture in real time, about an academic topic using semi-technical and technical vocabulary associated with the study of psychology. The response required, reproduced as Figure 2.1, is an outline of lecture notes recognizable as a legitimate academic task. This example is just one way computer technology can be used to provide rich visual and audio input for test takers, attempting to engage them in a situationally authentic, interactive assessment procedure.

Technology also opens the possibility for new test-task features and new test tasks such as the provision for instant access to help sources such as glossaries, dictionaries, or tutorials during examinee responses. For example, the TOEFL computer-based test (CBT) Reading Section, shown below as Figure 2.2, has a *help* button in the lower right corner of the screen that the test taker can click to see a screen that repeats the instructions for the section and allows for tutorials on specific test methods including how to scroll, test controls such as the *next, confirm, time,* and *volume* controls, and how to answer the specific task type, as shown in Figure 2.3.

The *How to Answer* button takes the test taker to a screen, as shown in

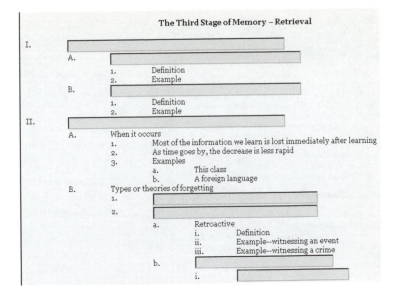

The Third Stage of Memory – Retrieval

I.

   A.
      1.   Definition
      2.   Example

   B.
      1.   Definition
      2.   Example

II.

   A.   When it occurs
      1.   Most of the information we learn is lost immediately after learning
      2.   As time goes by, the decrease is less rapid
      3.   Examples
         a.   This class
         b.   A foreign language
   B.   Types or theories of forgetting
      1.
      2.
         a.   Retroactive
            i.   Definition
            ii.   Example--witnessing an event
            iii.   Example--witnessing a crime
         b.
            i.

Figure 2.1 *WebLAS* listening response task
(http://www.humnet.ucla.edu/web/departments/alt/
weblas_esl_demo/demo_listen_out_psych1.htm).

Figure 2.4, that provides a tutorial on how to proceed with tasks requiring students to highlight segments of the text on the screen. Instant access to optional instructions and response information might offer a useful advantage to some test takers as the test developers intended. This example also shows a new type of test task afforded by technology.

The potential offered by such capabilities as contextualization, help, and new task types are not well understood or extensively used by test developers. As Fulcher (2000) has pointed out, test developers are justifiably concerned that the use of such multimedia and computer interactions may influence what is being measured because of the test – the "method effect" mentioned above – and test developers are quite naturally unwilling to go too far too fast in employing the full range of new test-task options in CALT without a more complete understanding of the consequences for test-taker performance and the interpretation of test results.

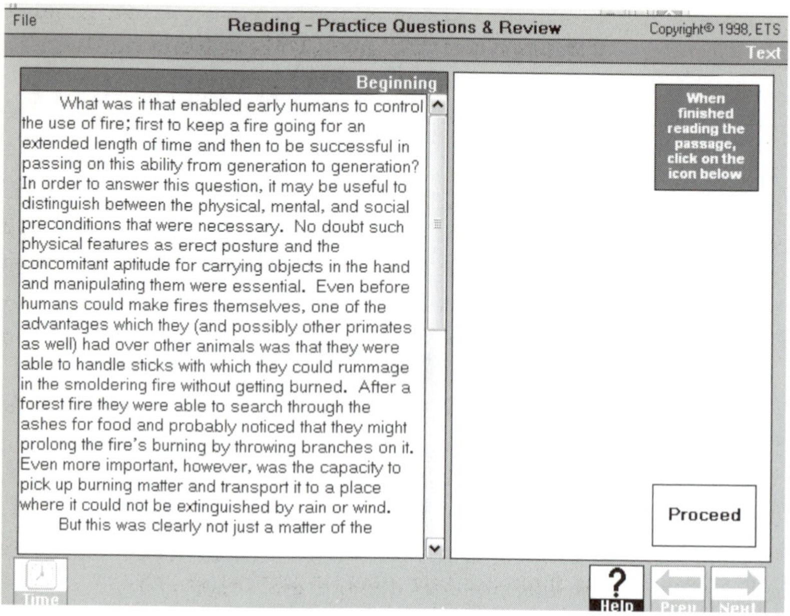

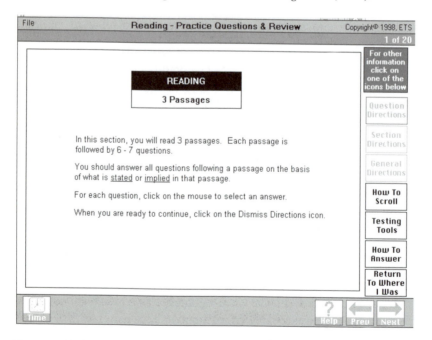

Figure 2.2 TOEFL CBT reading task (Educational Testing Service, 1999).

Figure 2.3 TOEFL CBT instruction screen (Educational Testing Service, 1999).

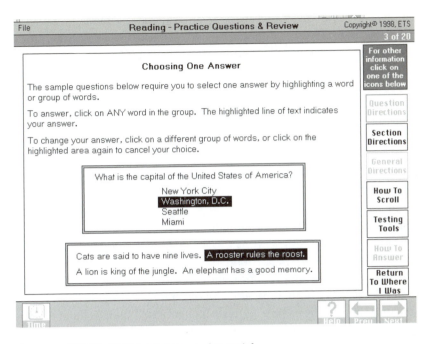

Figure 2.4 TOEFL CBT highlighting task tutorial
(Educational Testing Service, 1999).

Interaction between the input and response

CALT methods can affect the interaction between the input and response, with regard to *reactivity*, the way the input changes, or reacts, in light of the test taker's responses. In test formats such as live interviews, for example, which intend to reflect aspects of face-to-face conversation, the interviewer has many options for modifying the input, increasing or decreasing the level of difficulty of vocabulary or the complexity of syntax, for instance, if the test taker's performance indicates an ability level too high or low for the initial test task. The interviewer can also switch the topic to one that might be more compatible with the test taker's interests and purposes, and can elicit aspects of language use the test taker may be attempting to avoid. The experienced interviewer will also be sensitive to the test taker's apparent level of ability and make frequent "probes" for higher and lower ability levels, finally "zeroing-in" on an appropriate level at which the test taker can sustain the performance (see, for example, Liskin-Gasparro, 1984, for a description of the American

Council on the Teaching of Foreign Languages Oral Proficiency Interview).

This type of flexibility, or adaptivity, is not possible in test formats such as paper-and-pencil reading tests, or in tape-recorded listening tests, where the input is presented in a linear fashion and test takers must attempt all tasks, whether they are too easy or too difficult. It will be a long time before computer technology mirrors the flexibility of a good interviewer in an oral test. However, as we discussed in Chapter 1, CALT technology does allow for some degree of interaction between input and response in tests of listening or reading ability, or knowledge of grammatical structure. For such tests the computer's precision in evaluating responses and adapting accordingly arguably outperforms what a human tester would accomplish as accurately and reliably in practice.

Computer-adaptive tests (CATs) were made possible by the development in testing theory that extended beyond classical true score theory, which underlies traditional approaches to estimation of reliability and test item statistics (e.g., item difficulty). Item response theory (IRT) underlies statistical item analysis procedures which produce sample independent item statistics to estimate an item's difficulty and other parameters with respect to a test taker of a given ability. After analysis of pre-test data, each item is "tagged" with a given level of difficulty such that test takers from the same population as the pre-test sample have a 50% chance of getting the item correct. A number of large-scale language tests employ IRT/CAT techniques to at least some degree, including DIALANG and TOEFL. IRT-based CATs are particularly well suited for tests consisting of a set of independent items, but a variation has been used for assessing skills that require relatively large amounts of text as input, such as listening or reading. Although examples of one-item-per-passage reading tests exist (e.g., Choi, Kim, & Boo, 2003), item-level adaptivity is typically seen as inefficient and impractical if test takers have to spend several minutes reading for each item they complete on the test. Therefore, text-and-question sets, called *testlets*, are constructed, each set representing a different level of ability (Bradlow, Wainer & Wang, 1999). During the test, rather than selecting individual items based on correct or incorrect responses to previous items, the computer selects entire passages and associated questions. For example, the ACT Placement Test, developed by ACT, Inc. (formerly called the American College Test, Incorporated), comprises three modules – Grammar/Usage, Reading, and Listening – which can be administered individually or in combination, with each test generating a separate placement score. A testlet from the Grammar/Usage test is illustrated in Figure 2.5.

Level 4

Item Types: (1) Passive voice verbs; (2) Punctuation conventions: parentheticals; (3) Conjunctions; (4) Noun clauses; (5) Noun clauses

The lion **(1)** _____ the "king of beasts," but in fact, this king doesn't do much to deserve the title. Lions live in groups; each group, or "pride," of lions consists of one dominant male and several females and their offspring. However, all the **(2)** _____ is done by the lionesses, the females. Males spend their time **(3)** _____ what they have killed. Occasionally, males may have to scare off possible threats to the group, but for no more effort than this, they get to eat first, and to eat until they are full. Male lions are also guilty of what **(4)** _____ not very kingly behavior. When a new male takes over the pride, he will usually kill all the cubs of the male that formerly led the pride. This ensures that only his own offspring will survive. This may seem brutal, but it is how **(5)** _____. Perhaps we might want to reconsider calling the lion the "king of beasts."

1.
- ☐ **A.** is often been calling
- ☐ **B.** has often called
- ☐ **C.** is often been called
- ☑ **D.** has often been called

2.
- ☑ **A.** work—the stalking, chasing, and killing of prey—
- ☐ **B.** work—the stalking, chasing, and killing of prey:
- ☐ **C.** work;—the stalking, chasing, and killing of prey;
- ☐ **D.** work:—the stalking, chasing, and killing of prey

3.
- ☑ **A.** either sleeping while the females hunt or eating
- ☐ **B.** sleeping while either the females hunting or eat
- ☐ **C.** either sleeping while the females hunt or eat
- ☐ **D.** sleeping while the females either hunt or eating

4.
- ☐ **A.** would we probably call
- ☑ **B.** we would probably call
- ☐ **C.** we would probably call it
- ☐ **D.** would we probably called

5.
- ☐ **A.** nature does working
- ☐ **B.** is nature working
- ☑ **C.** nature works
- ☐ **D.** does nature work

Figure 2.5 ACT Placement Test Grammar/Usage testlet
(ACT, 2004).

In this example set, the text and the questions associated with it are presented as a package and the test taker's performance on the set will determine the ability level of the next set presented in the test. In view of the need to include connected discourse as the input on language tests, testlets offer an added dimension to the use of CATs for language assessment.

Despite the fact that CATs do not offer the same type of adaptivity as live interactive techniques such as interviews can, they offer many advantages over more static methods in the measurement of certain language abilities. However, they also pose challenges to test developers, particularly in ensuring adequate coverage of a range of content, and ensuring that a range of language tasks are presented that adequately represent the abilities intended to be measured. In order to make certain that a wide range of content and ability levels is covered, CATs require that a very large number of items be created and pre-tested, and this makes test construction very time consuming and expensive. In addition, the adaptive algorithm, or the rules by which the computer selects each item for presentation, must be carefully constructed to ensure that, in addition to the difficulty of the item with respect to a test taker at a given ability level, the algorithm is sensitive to such factors as linguistic and topical content and task type as well. The challenge of developing computer-adaptive language tests that reflect the need to assess communicative language ability will occupy language test developers and researchers for decades to come. For example, in the future, computers may be able to make use of spoken input in an adaptive manner, thus emulating features of human spoken interaction in a way unheard of at the present time.

Characteristics of assessment

Computers have long been used to score certain types of test tasks: the IBM Model 805 Test Scoring Machine (see Figure 2.6), introduced in 1935, could score "objective" tests ten times faster than humans, and with greater accuracy. This concept is still in use today, essentially unchanged except with respect to advances in computer technology itself, and the arguments, pro and con, about the use of multiple-choice tests are also little changed from those of 80 years ago (Fulcher, 2000). Suffice it to say that when it comes to scoring multiple-choice tests, the differences between human and machine are speed and accuracy. In the rating of complex written or spoken production tasks, however, the differences between humans and machines are more complex and worthy of investigation. Three aspects of the assessment component of test method characteristics are relevant: the definition of the aspect of language being measured, the criteria by which the performance will be evaluated, and the procedure by which the performance will be scored.

To rate a written or spoken response to a prompt, humans syntactically parse the text, interpret vocabulary and larger semantic units, analyze the larger discourse of the response, assigning it a pragmatic interpretation, and compare it to a set of formal criteria for determining quality, all within a set of constraints established by the communicative context. In

Figure 2.6   IBM Model 805 Test Scoring Machine
            (IBM Corporation, 2002).

view of the complexity of this process, training the personnel necessary
for rating language in tests presents a challenge for research and practice.
In order to help ensure consistency in scoring complex language performances, precise scoring rubrics must be developed and raters must be
trained to use them reliably and efficiently. The larger the testing
program, the more raters are needed and the more costly the operation
becomes. It is no wonder that when short answers or extended responses
are called for in a language test, whether written, as in cloze or essay tasks,
or spoken, as in pronunciation or simulated oral interview tasks, computer scoring and response analysis is an attractive prospect. To rate
spoken and written language by computer, relatively complex technologies of speech recognition, parsing, and discourse analysis are required.
Some progress has been made in applying these to language assessment,
and we can therefore consider in more depth the two examples mentioned in the previous chapter, Criterion, and PhonePass SET-10.

Criterion

The Educational Testing Service, the organization that produces TOEFL
as well as a number of other academic and professional tests, has developed an automated system known as Criterion for rating extended

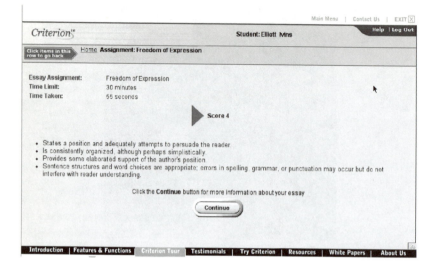

Figure 2.7 An example of a Criterion report (Educational Testing Service, 2005b).

written responses. Criterion employs NLP techniques to syntactically parse textual input, assigning grammatical labels to items, and looking for markers of discourse structure and content vocabulary items. It is employed in the online service which provides writing evaluation and feedback to students and instructors (Educational Testing Service, 2005a). Criterion can assign a holistic rating to an essay on a six-point scale, as shown in the online example of a Criterion report in Figure 2.7. The commentary associated with the rating is based on aspects of NLP analysis such as that derived from another ETS product, *e-rater* (Monaghan and Bridgeman 2005), which analyzes seven categories of features: grammar mechanics (e.g., spelling), usage (e.g., article errors), style (e.g., overly repeated words, extremely long sentences), level of vocabulary used, organization/development (e.g., identification of sentences corresponding to the background, thesis, main idea, supporting idea, and conclusion), and prompt-specific vocabulary usage. According to research conducted at ETS, e-rater can also serve as a backup to a human rater rather than as a stand-alone automated essay scoring tool (Monaghan and Bridgeman 2005). For example, a human rater and e-rater both rate an essay; if their scores agree closely, the final score is the single human rating; if the scores are not close, a second human rater adjudicates the discrepancy (human and computer language rating

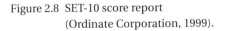

PhonePass   **Score Report**   **Spoken English Test**

Test: SET-10 (24.33.43)
Test Paper Number: 66114742
Administration data: 06 JAN 1999, 20:05 – 20:15 (PST)

		2	3	4	5	6	7	8
OVERALL	**6.9**							
Listening Vocabulary	6.3							
Repeat Accuracy	6.6							
Pronunciation	8.0							
Reading Fluency	7.3							
Repeat Fluency	7.0							

Figure 2.8 SET-10 score report
(Ordinate Corporation, 1999).

comparisons are discussed in the next chapter). Monaghan and Bridgeman found that in the latter case, a second human rating was needed about 15% of the time, and that using e-rater as a check in this way produced scores that were within a half-point (on a six-point scale) of an independent criterion score 75.5% of the time and within one point 93.9% of the time. The basic e-rater technology is a promising development and research is continuing to further enhance its usefulness.

PhonePass SET-10

SET-10 (formerly known as PhonePass), a computer-scored test of spoken English for non-native speakers, developed by Ordinate, Inc., also makes use of NLP technology. Test takers are given a printed set of instructions, and then contact the computer by telephone, to receive additional oral instructions. They provide their oral responses over the telephone and then these are rated by computer. The test contains a variety of task types, including sentence reading, sentence repetition, and word pronunciation prompted by semantic opposites and by either/or questions. Actual items are drawn randomly for each administration from a large pool of pre-tested items. Results are reported on the Web, as illustrated in Figure 2.8.

The SET-10 rating procedure is based on a speech recognition system containing an algorithm derived from the study of a large spoken corpus of native speaker language representing various English regional and social dialects. It compares test taker performances with a template representing specific elicited vocabulary, phonetic features of consonants and vowels, as well as phrasing and timing of sentences. The rating program has been subjected to extensive study and has been shown to correlate at .94 with human raters for the overall rating and between .79 and .89 for the subscores (Ordinate Corporation, 2002a). The SET-10 system is a stand-alone rating program that operates without human intervention, although it is carefully monitored by the program administration.

Another way to exploit the capabilities of computer technology to assist the rating process is to provide various types of easily accessible help for raters. For example, the developers of the Oral English Proficiency Test at Purdue University are working on a computer-based rater system that will present the test item on screen and include an option to play benchmark responses for any of the tasks as the human raters work through the test responses (Ginther, 2001, personal communication). Rater performance will be automatically monitored and problematic items and raters flagged. The intent is that this system will help to maintain the standards set by the developers. Similarly, the Computerized Oral Proficiency Instrument (COPI), developed at the Center for Applied Linguistics (Malabonga, Kenyon & Carpenter, 2002), employs computer-mediated scoring that allows raters to listen to test-taker responses online, automatically tabulates scores according to an algorithm, and stores test taker responses and ratings. Both these initiatives appear to be promising approaches to combining the capabilities of computer and human raters to evaluate constructed responses.

The potential for the automated scoring of constructed response tasks is one of the more exciting promises of CALT because of the potential it holds for increasing the practicality of constructed response language test tasks. In view of this obvious potential, research is needed to better understand the limitations of NLP, particularly its consequences for understanding the constructs that we attempt to measure. Automated scoring is clearly different from human scoring, but the challenge is to understand under what circumstances it is more useful than human scorers for rating test takers' language production.

Conclusion

This chapter has examined the ways in which computer technology expands the test developer's options for constructing language test tasks. Several examples illustrated ways in which computer-assisted language tests are different in fundamental ways for test takers, test developers, teachers, and researchers from other test delivery formats. Differences provided by CALT affect more than efficiency in the service of testing more people faster, getting tests scored and reporting results more quickly and cheaply. Computer-assisted language tests are different from other types of language tests in the method characteristics of the input and response, the interaction between them, and assessment. The rich contextualized input, the variety of response techniques, computer adaptivity, and automated scoring made possible by computer require careful consideration of the aspects of language the test developer intends to measure and the features of the target language use situation.

In focusing on the opportunities afforded by technology, this chapter only mentioned some of the caveats that must accompany consideration of computer-assisted language testing, including security issues for high-stakes tests, the level of technical expertise, and standardization and maintenance of equipment necessary; the potential for detracting from consistency that accompanies the computer's capability for providing different levels and languages of instructions, help screens, and input and response formats; and current restrictions on the computer's ability to emulate natural language processing and interaction. The following chapter expands on these issues from the perspective of how they affect the validity of inferences and uses of CALT.

CHAPTER THREE

The threat of CALT

The new options that technology offers for language test tasks present teachers, test developers, and researchers with an expanded set of possibilities for assessing language ability. At the same time, however, these options raise questions about what the new tests actually measure and what test scores from CALT can be used for. In our experience, the mention of technology for language assessment prompts skeptical comments from teachers, test developers, and researchers. One language-testing researcher characterized the skepticism by writing about the potential threats of computer-assisted language testing in addition to the promises. Expanding on the promises, Chapter 2 discussed the new options afforded by computer technology within the framework of the test method characteristics. This chapter examines the threats by making explicit connections between concerns about technology in language testing and validity. Some concerns about CALT that we mentioned in Chapter 2 pertain to (1) the inferences that can be drawn from test scores on computer-based tests and (2) the uses of the scores for purposes such as certification, admissions decisions, assigning grades, and advising learners. These two validity issues form the basis of at least six concerns that are often expressed as potential threats to CALT. In this chapter, we identify these potential threats and explain the ways in which research might address them. The fact that this chapter raises more questions than answers reflects the status of knowledge about inferences and uses of CALT, but identification of these issues is a first step to progress in this area.

The potential threats to the validity of inferences and uses of CALT are summarized in Table 3.1. The list appearing in the left column was developed from our synthesis of comments and concerns expressed by students, teachers, test developers, and researchers as they have been gradually introduced to CALT over the past 20 years. Some of these, such as test security, have received attention in the public discourse on assessment whereas others such as scoring linguistic responses have come up in less public arenas such as committees concerned with test development, and research projects. Despite their origins, each potential

Table 3.1 *Potential threats to the validity of CALT*

Potential threat to validity	Approaches for addressing threat
Different test performance. Performance on a computer-delivered test may fail to reflect the same ability as that which would be measured by other forms of assessment.	Mode comparison validation studies Comparison of contrasting group Investigation of computer-method effects
New task types. The types of items that can be developed in computer-assisted formats are different from those that can be developed with other media.	Investigation of new item types
Limitations due to adaptive item selection. Selection of items to be included on an adaptive test by an algorithm may not result in an appropriate sample of test content and may cause test takers anxiety.	Exploration of approaches other than item-level adaptivity Experimentation with variations in item presentation and control
Inaccurate automatic response scoring. Computer-assisted response scoring may fail to assign credit to the qualities of a response that are relevant to the construct that the test is intended to measure.	Application of multifaceted, relevant criteria for evaluating machine scoring Comparison of detailed (partial-credit) scoring with other methods Comparison of machine and human ratings Development of appropriate (construct-relevant) scoring criteria
Compromised security. CALT may pose risks to test security.	Investigation of appropriate pool-size for computer-adaptive test items Establishment of testing centers Use of advanced technologies for identification
Negative consequences. CALT may have negative impact on learners, learning, classes, and society.	Careful planning and budgeting Preparation of learners for computer-based testing Investigation of washback

threat is relevant to anyone interested in the future of language assessment because these issues will play a central role in research and practice.

Different test performance

Perhaps the most ubiquitous concern raised about technology for language assessment is that examinees' performance on a CALT may fail to reflect the same ability as that which is measured by other forms of assessment. The potential problem concerns the inferences that can be made about examinees' ability on the basis of their test performance. Of course, if a computer-based test results in a score meaning which is different from that of an otherwise similar paper-and-pencil test, it is a threat only to the extent that score users intend the two scores to be equivalent. This unstated intention typically underlies discussion of the potential threat, and therefore, one way the problem has been expressed by educational measurement specialists is the following: "If the fact that items are presented on a computer screen, rather than on a piece of paper, changes the mental processes required to respond correctly to the item, the validity of the inferences based on these scores may be changed" (Wainer, Dorans, Eignor, Flaugher, Green, Mislevy, Steinberg & Thissen, 2000, p. 16).

The comparison refers to a computer-delivered test vs. one delivered through any other format, whether it be paper-and-pencil, a face-to-face interview, or a cassette-recorded monologue. This concern for all computer-based tests is relevant to second language tests, which typically require the examinee to read and manipulate texts on the computer screen or attend to a combination of sounds and images presented as test input, as illustrated in the previous chapter. Over 15 years ago, one of the pioneers in computer-based testing outlined a number of possible reasons for expecting different test performance on a computer-based test; reasons included differences in ease of backtracking, screen capacity, ease of response, and use of individually controlled time limits (Green, 1988). Some of these particulars would be different today, in part because of changes in technology, but also because of examinees' greater familiarity with computer use.

However, even if examinees are accustomed to looking for information on the Internet and using a word-processing program, they may find that manipulating and controlling the computer through their second language poses challenges that critics would claim are more computer-related than language ability-related. For example, examinees who take a grammar test requiring them to click on phrases and drag them to the correct position to make a sentence may not know how to manipulate this type of item if they have never worked with it prior to taking the test. In a test situation, this lack of familiarity might result in shaken confidence that could negatively affect the performance on the task despite a strong knowledge of grammar. Or more seriously, it could result in a set of uncompleted items because of time lost in attempting to figure out how to respond. In either case, the inference made from the test score would be that the examinee did not have strong grammatical competence, whereas the correct inference would be that the examinee did not have competence in completing click and drag items. The general issue – that the computer mode of delivery may affect performance – should be of critical interest for those who investigate all types of language tests. A number of methods can be used to address this issue, but examination of the few examples of research indicates that developers of computer-based language tests have seldom investigated what seems to be a critical question.

Test comparison studies

Perhaps the most obvious way of investigating the question of whether examinees perform well on a computer-based test for the wrong reason (i.e., differential test performance due to factors other than differences in the ability to be measured) is through a study that compares examinees' performance on two tests which are the same except for the mode of delivery, i.e., one form of the test is delivered as a paper-and-pencil test and the other is delivered by computer. Among the first large testing programs in the United States to transform their tests to computer-based testing, the Graduate Record Examination (GRE) conducted a number of comparisons on test items, sections, and total test scores in a research program intended to investigate the comparability of the computer-based and paper-and-pencil forms of the GRE. In several studies which obtained test performance data from examinees who had taken both computer-based forms and paper-and-pencil versions of the GRE, researchers found very few and slight differences that they thought might warrant further investigation of mode effects, but they did not find overall clear and consistent mode effects that would indicate that different inferences should be made from the two forms of the GRE (Schaeffer, Reese, Steffen, McKinley & Mills, 1993).

The GRE has a section assessing verbal ability, but more pertinent to CALT issues was the research conducted on the TOEFL to provide data about the similarity between the paper-and-pencil version and the types of tasks that would be used on the computer-based TOEFL, which was introduced in 1998 (Taylor, Kirsch, Eignor & Jamieson, 1999). Students took the two versions of the TOEFL, the computer-delivered and paper-and-pencil TOEFL; the researchers found a correlation of .84 between the two. Even though this is not a particularly strong correlation if it is interpreted as a parallel forms reliability coefficient, the researchers interpreted it as indicating that the effects of computer delivery did not strongly affect what was tested. However, the interpretation one can make from a bivariate correlation of two similar language tests is limited. In order to attempt to isolate how features of the test task might influence performance, one might hope for the type of research conducted for the GRE – a closer comparison of computer-delivered and traditional items that were intended to assess the same language abilities. An example of one such study examined the difference in performance on a listening test with audio-only and audio-with-video input (Coniam, 2001). No notable quantitative differences between the two modes were found in this case, but the question is worthy of further investigation.

Another study examined comparability using a range of empirical methods that offered complementary perspectives. Choi, Kim, and Boo (2003) sought evidence pertaining to comparability of the paper-based language test and the computer version of the Test of English Proficiency developed by Seoul National University through the use of content analysis, correlational analyses, ANOVA, and confirmatory factor analysis. Findings indicted strong similarities between the two versions (PPT and CBT) of each of the different parts of the test, with the grammar sections displaying the greatest similarities and the reading section displaying the largest disparities.

On the surface, findings of no notable differences between test formats should satisfy users that language test scores are not strongly influenced by computer delivery. However, careful consideration of such findings raises several questions. First, if the computer delivery produces an essentially equivalent test, is it worth the cost of changing the test format? If the computer-delivered test is to be more efficient, is efficiency a sufficient reason? Shouldn't a *better* test be the goal? After the test developer invests the time and money in producing a listening test with video, for example, we would hope that the resulting test scores are better indicators of the listening ability that the test intends to measure than the test with audio alone. Second, is the contribution to test scores that might come from examinees' ability to manipulate the computer really irrelevant to their language ability, as it should be defined in the twenty-first century? For example, if students arriving at a university in the United States are unable to navigate and input their responses into the computer-based test intended for placement, WebLAS, are they well prepared for using English in an academic setting in the United States, where both procedural administrative matters and scholarship take place in part through interaction with technology? Third, should an overall finding of similarity between the two forms be assumed to indicate that a small minority of individuals who have little experience in using computers are not disadvantaged by the delivery? The first two issues will be taken up in subsequent chapters whereas the third is addressed by research comparing test performance across groups.

Contrasting group studies

Contrasting groups have been used to investigate whether those individuals with little experience using computers are disadvantaged when they take a computer-delivered test. Such a disadvantage might show up as a lower than expected correlation between computer-based and paper-and-pencil tests within a larger group; however, such a finding could not be attributed to a disadvantage for particular individuals. Steinberg, Thissen, and Wainer (2000) refer to the potential problem as "differential validity":

> It is conceivable that a [computer-based test] may be more vulnerable to problems of differential validity than are conventional paper-and-pencil tests, due to the possibility that differences between ethnic groups or genders in familiarity with computers in general may affect scores on computerized tests.   (p. 204)

In international L2 testing this is potentially an important issue, as some members of the international population may have had less experience in using computers than others. Research investigating the computer familiarity of over 100,000 ESL test takers internationally in 1997 found distinct differences by region, with 5.6% of the 27,988 survey respondents in the United States and Canada reporting having never used a computer and 24.5% of the 1,650 surveyed in Africa reporting the same (Taylor, Jamieson, & Eignor, 2000). It should be noted that the survey was

conducted on examinees who were intending to study in higher education in the United States or Canada, and therefore results do not general-
ize to the total population in either region. Although some see prospects
for the rapid spread of technology use, it seems reasonable to expect that
regional differences will remain for the foreseeable future and this
expectation is supported by global data sources such as GeoHive (2005).

Despite the potential significance of differential validity, to date not a
single study of L2 testing has examined directly whether or not past experience with computers affects test performance on a computer-based L2 test.
The TOEFL computer familiarity study, however, did provide some data that
are pertinent to the issue (Taylor et al., 1999). The test takers in the study
were assigned to groups on the basis of their responses to a questionnaire
asking them to estimate their level of knowledge and amount of use of computer applications such as word processing and Internet. The scores of the
two groups were then compared to determine the extent to which computer
familiarity affected performance on the computer-delivered test. In doing
the comparison of the groups, the researchers included the scores on the
paper-and-pencil TOEFL to account for language ability as measured
without influence of the computer medium. After accounting for language
ability (as measured by the paper-and-pencil TOEFL), no meaningful
difference between performance of computer-familiar and computer-
unfamiliar participants on the computer-delivered test was found. On the
surface, this study appears to suggest that concerns about differential validity may be less of an issue than one might at first suppose.

However, the real purpose of the TOEFL computer familiarity study was
to determine whether practical differences were evident between the
groups after they had engaged in up to an hour of instruction on how to
use the computer. In other words, the intent was to see whether potential
effects of the differential past experience could be minimized through
completion of an online tutorial that would be available in testing centers
for operational testing (Jamieson, Taylor, Kirsch & Eignor, 1998). The
research design was not directed toward gaining data about the theoretical issue of differential validity, but instead was driven by the practical
reality that an administrative decision to move the TOEFL to computer
had already been made at the time of the research. Although the study
does not address the research question about the potential advantage of
prior computer experience, the practice-driven research design offers
some insight into the puzzling absence of comparison and differential
validity studies. This study reflects the sociological reality that decisions
about delivering a test by computer are generally made, as suggested in

Chapter 2, for reasons other than research findings that indicate no differences between performance on the computer-based test and the other form of the test. Technology is often chosen as the obvious means for developing new assessments, and one can speculate as to whether performance is affected measurably as a result. However, until research compares performance of novice and experienced computer users on language tests, it is not clear whether or not such speculation might be supported empirically. In view of the widespread use of technology, a finding of differences does not necessarily mean that CALT should be considered suspect, but from the scientific perspective of gaining an understanding of computer-mediated test performance, the question remains interesting.

Interpretation of computer-method effects

Whether or not computer delivery of language tests can be shown to affect test scores statistically, another approach to investigating performance on computer-based tests is to examine the test-taking process of examinees who are completing a language test (Cohen, 1998). Such research addresses in a qualitative fashion the suggestion that computer-delivery may affect "the mental processes required to respond correctly to the item," as Wainer et al. (2000) suggested. In a review of research on computer-based reading tests Sawaki (2001) concluded that to conduct such research "adequate process measures should be devised and included in empirical studies. Methodologies such as analysis of eye movement and verbal protocol analysis as well as post hoc interviews and questionnaires may be useful for this purpose" (p. 51). She points out that this type of research is conducted in human factors research (such as research informing interface design), and hypertext research, but that such studies do not appear in the research literature of second language testing (Sawaki, 2001). This is not to say that such research is not conducted, but only that it is not designed and formalized in a way that results in its publication in the public literature. Rather, these methods that have been used in other research, are also used in small-scale pilot studies during test design and development and therefore are not prepared for publication.

It may be that if the profession is to appreciate the significance of detailed results of studies explaining differences between CALT and other forms of tests, statistical differences need to be found in test scores. As both Sawaki's and Chalhoub-Deville and Deville's (1999) reviews of research on CALT point out, despite the many CALT projects, no published research has attempted to investigate questions of score comparability. Chalhoub-Deville and Deville conclude that "research in L2 is still scarce regarding the comparability of P&P and computer scores" (1999, p. 282). This conclusion may imply that comparability research is forthcoming, and indeed, some studies have appeared since then. However, considering that computer-based L2 testing has been going on for at least two decades, we have to question why such research has not played a more prominent role in test developers' agendas.

As mentioned above, it seems that testing programs do not make decisions about whether or not to develop a computer-based test on the basis of research results on performance differences. Then, what is to be learned from such results? Sawaki's summary of the research begins with the premise that the "presence of a [large] mode effect on reading comprehension test performance would seriously invalidate score interpretation of computerized reading tests" (Sawaki, 2001, p. 38). This perspective is consistent with research on test method effects in language testing, which is typically based on the assumption that the construct of interest (e.g., reading ability) can and should be conceptualized as a free-standing trait. In other words, test users are interested in examinees' ability to read anything, anywhere, and this ability should be inferable on the basis of test performance. This would imply that the construct of reading would not include the ability to navigate through a hypertext, for example, because such navigation would extend beyond reading ability. In the final chapter, we will suggest that the usefulness of the free-standing trait perspective and the "pure" construct is too limited for the many testing purposes and contexts of interest to test users, and therefore in order for test users to understand the promises and threats of CALT, they need to grasp how language constructs can be conceived from multiple perspectives as well as how technology intersects with construct definition.

New task types

A second set of potential threats to validity of the inferences and uses of CALT is related to test content issues resulting from the constraints the medium places on the types of tasks, or items, in the test. The problem is not unique to computer-based tests but is defined by the particulars of what test designers can and cannot do with the medium used to construct tasks. For example, the Purdue ITA speaking test includes many different tasks for the examinee to complete, including speaking from written text prompts as well as listening to and responding to a speaker who is shown on video. The test offers an impressive array of tasks; at the same time they are constrained by the fact that the computer was chosen as a vehicle for presentation. Tasks one might wish to consider but that are not conducive to the medium would include presentation of a mini-lesson, or participation in a simulated office hours session.

At a more micro level, one might also question the way in which particulars of the screen and the interface affect the way that items are constructed by the test writers and interpreted by test takers. For example, the TOEFL reading item that requests examinees to identify the location for an additional sentence in the paragraph allows the examinee to see a nine-sentence paragraph. If the paragraph had been longer, test writers would have had to shorten it to fit on the screen with the same size font. The same issue of physical size for extended texts arises for any reading test, but the limits of space are met sooner when the text is on a computer screen. In a reading test intended to measure discourse comprehension or scanning, a longer text is needed, and therefore, the examinee must scroll or move from page to page. In either case the test taker never sees the complete text on the screen. The specific constraints are largely defined by the software and design decisions made at a higher level than any particular item. For example, a particular font size is typically chosen to achieve a certain look and consistency among the parts of the software. A host of other decisions have to be made during the authoring process including such details as the placement of images, access to audio, amount displayed on a screen, and access to previous texts and items. These issues are ideally addressed by examining the influence of particular item types on test takers' strategies and performance through qualitative research.

Limitations due to adaptive item selection

Computer-adaptive testing has been the most salient form of CALT over the past 20 years and therefore has been the subject of some research. As illustrated in Chapter 2 through the ACT ESL Placement Test, the adaptive selection of test items results in a shorter test than what could be offered without the adaptivity, assuming a comparable reliability. At the same time, questions have been raised concerning the effect of leaving item selection up to a computer program that chooses items on the basis of the level of difficulty of the items. From the time that the first examples of computer-adaptive language tests began to appear, Canale (1986) raised the possibility that the computer-adaptive paradigm would be potentially "trivializing," "compromising," and "reductionist" (Canale, 1986, pp. 34–5). Early developers of computer-adaptive tests created an item pool by sampling from many aspects of the construct of interest, but then items were selected from the pool for any given examinee on the basis of statistical characteristics alone, i.e., without considering whether or not the examinee was taking a test that sampled appropriately from the relevant content. If the content of such a test is left to chance, an ESL grammar test administered to an advanced-level examinee, for example, might choose all items targeting knowledge of noun clauses, such as the one shown in Figure 3.1.

Although word order within complex noun phrases is an appropriate advanced-level grammar item, a test of English grammar must sample across a range of structures in order for test scores to be valid as indicators of grammatical knowledge. The way that the "Male lion. . ." item is actually presented in the ACT ESL test illustrates one approach to the problem of test content in an adaptive test: rather than having the item-selection algorithm choose each item individually, items are clustered so that advanced-level noun phrase items are presented in a passage along with advanced-level items testing passive voice verbs, punctuation conventions, parentheticals, and conjunctions, as illustrated in Chapter 2. By presenting items in bundles, or "testlets" (Wainer et al., 2000), the test designer gains more control over the way content is sampled.

A second approach to this issue is to tag individual items in a pool with information about content and to have the item-selection algorithm

---

Male lions are also guilty of what (4) _____ not very kingly behavior.

A. would we probably call

B. we would probably call

C. we would probably call it

D. would we probably called

Figure 3.1 One item from the grammar test of the ACT ESL test
(from: http://www.act.org/esl/sample/grammar4.html).

choose test items on the basis of content as well as statistical properties. However, in view of the desirability for language test items to be constructed from connected text, rather than from individual words or sentences, the testlet approach seems to hold the most promise, and therefore, this is an active research area. Early reports of computer-adaptive tests for reading illustrate the problem posed by the use of independent items. Madsen (1991), for example, reported on a computer-adaptive ESL test with items requiring examinees to read a one- to three-sentence prompt so that they could complete a sufficient number of items in a short amount of time, and so that the psychometric assumptions of the item-selection algorithm would be met. The assumptions were met, however, at the expense of assessing some aspects of the construct of reading comprehension, such as rhetorical competence or comprehension of the main idea of a passage. This is one type of reductionism that Canale (1986) was concerned with.

Adaptive tests have been used widely enough for research that concerns about the validity of test scores have been identified beyond those associated with test content. Another of the most salient is the observation that examinees become anxious as the item selection appears to present them continually with what they perceive to be difficult items under conditions where they cannot review and change responses. This observation seems contrary to claims by proponents of CAT that examinees should feel satisfied by the choice of items tailored to their level. In studies of first language (L1) vocabulary tests, researchers have explored the effects on anxiety, test time, and performance of giving examinees variations on the standard computer-adaptive format. In particular, experiments included a self-adaptive test (requiring the examinees themselves to decide whether each item should be the same, more difficult, or easier than the previous one) and tests providing feedback after each response. In both types of tests, provision for feedback after each item resulted in shorter time periods for both computer-adaptive and self-adaptive tests than their counterparts with no feedback, presumably because the feedback provided an impetus for more continuous concentration (Vispoel, 1998). Another study found that examinees tended to improve their answers when they had the opportunity to do so by being allowed to review, and that they report greater satisfaction when this option is available (Vispoel, Hendrickson & Bleiler, 2000). These attempts to better understand and address threats to the validity of computer-adaptive testing seek ways of modifying the canonical forms of the measurement technique to respond to the content tested and the examinees' feelings.

Inaccurate automatic response scoring

A fourth potential threat to the validity of CALT is evident in tests requiring examinees to solve a more complex task. Chapter 2 hints at the complex tasks that can be constructed when computer-assisted response analysis can be counted upon to score responses accurately. One example is the table-completion task included in the TOEFL reading section; others are the essay and speaking tasks on the GRE analytic writing section, and SET-10 (Ordinate Corporation, 2002b), respectively. The TOEFL reading item illustrates a task which allows a large but finite number of arrangements of elements in the table, whereas the GRE writing and SET-10 require linguistic constructed responses and therefore might, theoretically, elicit an infinite number of responses. In either case, when the examinee's response is complex, the potential danger for validity is that the computer scoring program may fail to assess the relevant and significant qualities of the response, and therefore award a higher or lower score than that which should be given, or that it might record erroneous diagnostic information about the examinee. A few studies begin to illustrate the complexity of developing a justifiable algorithm for scoring complex constructed responses.

Non-linguistic complex responses

In a study of a task intended to assess the ability to recognize the structure of a text, which Alderson, Percsich, and Szabo (2000) defined as one aspect of reading ability, decisions had to be made about the best way of scoring a text sequencing task, which required examinees to put the sentences in the correct order in a text whose sentences had been scrambled. Such a task, which adds significantly to the types of complex tasks that can be included on a language test, can yield a large but finite number of different answers. Even though only one response (i.e., one sequence of sentences) is considered by the examiners to be completely correct, all other responses are not necessarily completely incorrect. Examinees may place five out of six sentences correctly, for example, or they may place only two sentences in the correct sequential order, having recognized a cohesive signal between the pair. The researchers argue that scoring such a task dichotomously (i.e., with 0 for incorrect and 1 for correct) fails to reflect the construct accurately, and therefore a means of accurately scoring the task polytomously (i.e., with a range of scores) is needed.

The researchers had to decide upon the best computer algorithm for deriving polytomous scores for responses to the sequencing task. They did so by examining correlations between the text-sequencing task scores (calculated several different ways) and scores on other language tests, finding overall, that the dichotomously scored tasks produced scores that correlated slightly more highly with the other language tests. Does this mean that the dichotomously scored items were better after all? The authors do not draw that conclusion; instead, they pointed out that "correlations alone do not tell the whole story" (p. 443) in part because the criterion tests cannot tell the whole story. They end up drawing on the construct-related argument that prompted the research in the first place: "low scores on exact match [i.e., dichotomous] scores alone do not necessarily reflect a lack of ability to detect coherence in text, and therefore partial credit procedures are justified" (p. 443). This study illustrated the complexity of deciding how to score the responses and then how to evaluate the scoring methods. The solution in this case forecasts what we predict will be an evolving theme of such research: evaluation of complex, detailed analysis cannot be accomplished by correlating results obtained through these sensitive methods with those obtained from more crude measures, and therefore other means of evaluation are needed.

Linguistic responses

The complexity of the issue is even more apparent in language tests requiring the examinee to respond to test items by producing linguistic responses. Attempts to develop a computer program to score L1 English essays through quantifying linguistic features met with very limited success in the twentieth century (Wresch, 1993). Similarly, when this approach has been explored for ESL writing, results have been at least equally disappointing. One such study investigated the use of a text analysis program, Writer's Workbench, for evaluation of ESL learners' essays, finding that the quantitative measures (essay length, average word length, Kincaid readability, percent of complex sentences, percent of content words) correlated positively with holistic scores on ESL compositions (Reid, 1986). However, the correlations ranged only from .57 for essay length to .15 for percent of content words. To the extent that the holistic score is considered to provide a good indicator of writing ability, these correlations would not justify these computer-assisted scoring methods for this purpose.

Recent research on automatic scoring of L1 essays has applied a more sophisticated understanding of writing performance as well as modern NLP techniques. In addition, the research investigating the quality of the ratings extends beyond correlations with holistic ratings. E-Rater, which was discussed in the previous chapter, derives an essay score from its evaluation of three clusters of essay features: sentence syntax, organization (indicated through discourse features such as cohesive expressions), and content (indicated through vocabulary related to the specific topic prompted for the essay). The values on each of these variables that should be associated with a particular holistic score for a particular essay topic are calibrated on the basis of sample essays that have been scored by human raters. The evaluation of the scoring program included correlations with scores given by human raters (which were found to be strong), but also through evaluation of essays written specifically to cause the scoring program to fail. The features of the essays that cause failure are then used to improve the scoring program (Powers, Burstein, Chodorow, Fowles & Kukich, 2001).

The same issue, but on a different scale, is evident in language tests requiring the examinee to produce short constructed responses such as a fraction of a word, a phrase, or a single sentence. In the 1960s and 1970s researchers investigated the effects of different scoring methods for cloze test responses consisting of single words that examinees write into blanks in passages. Occurring before computers were widely available for language testing, this research was intended primarily for justifying the use of an exact word dichotomous scoring method by showing its equivalence to more complex methods that would require raters to make judgments about the closeness of the test taker's response to the precise word that had been deleted. Oller (1979) begins his summary of the results of this research with the thesis that "all of the scoring methods that have ever been investigated produce highly correlated measures" (p. 367), and he concludes that "except for special research purposes there is probably little to be gained by using a complex weighting scale for degrees of appropriateness in scoring cloze tests" (p. 373). This conclusion was not universally agreed upon by language-testing researchers (e.g., Alderson, 1980). Moreover, this conclusion (based on correlational evidence) was drawn at a time when the process of response analysis was conducted by human raters and evaluated on the basis of corrrelational evidence. Perhaps because automatic response analysis was not a practical option, the possibility of expanding potential interpretations from test scores through detailed analysis was only mentioned as a postscript. Today, it seems that these issues need to be reopened in earnest to explore the potential of these short linguistic responses for learners and test users.

More recently similar types of items are seen in the outline completion tasks in the reading and listening tests of WebLAS shown in Chapter 2 as well as the WebLAS gap-filling test. The research on response scoring in WebLAS has not yet been published, but a few studies have explored the scoring of these types of items on different tests. One investigated an ESL reading test requiring examinees to produce short phrases and sentences in response to open-ended questions about reading passages (Henning, Anbar, Helm & D'Arcy, 1993). The researchers used a computer program to assign scores to responses, giving partial credit for partially correct responses because, like Alderson et al. (2004), they were concerned that the scoring method should accurately capture what the examinees knew. The researchers attempted to assess whether the effort of analyzing responses and assigning partial scores had allowed them to assess reading comprehension differently than when the responses were scored dichotomously. They examined the difference between the dichotomous and polytomous scoring methods by calculating correlations of scores from each method with the scores that had been obtained on a set of multiple-choice questions about the same passage. The scores derived from dichotomously scored, open-ended items produced higher correlations with the multiple-choice test scores (r=.99) than those from the polytomously-scored, open-ended items did (r=.89). This indicated that when open-ended items were polytomously scored, the resulting test score captured a somewhat different ability from the score produced from the multiple-choice items. These results do not address the question of which scoring method produced the better reading test for its intended purpose, but they do show that the scoring method made a small difference. Other methods for examining responses or examinees' response processes would be needed to shed light on the meaning of the differences.

A study of automatic response recognition in a dictation test task looked at the problem more qualitatively. Coniam (1998) provided an example of how the scoring algorithm would evaluate a phrase such as the one a test taker wrote for the phrase "which needed to be typed in" in a dictation test. The test taker who wrote "which are needing to be typing" should be given a partial score for that response, he argued. The scoring program does this. But the question is, exactly how much credit should be given to that response and why? Should a score for this response be the same as "that needs to be typed" or "which needs typing" or "which needle to eyed"? Coniam recognized the absence of a clear rationale for assignment of partial scores, calling the scoring algorithm "to an extent, unprincipled: 'which are needing to be typing' as the answer scores 42% while 'which are needly to be typest' scores 33%, although the latter is arguably much more incoherent" (Coniam, 1998, p. 44).

A principled approach to scoring constructed linguistic responses must rely on a theory of the construct that the test is intended to measure. Another study discussing the detail of a scoring algorithm for constructed responses demonstrated how the theory of what was being measured was used to assign set values for particular responses. Jamieson, Campbell, Norfleet and Berbisada (1993) designed a scoring program to assess the examinees' responses in the same way that human raters would, and in a way that systematically reflected the relative value of potential responses in view of construct theory. The linguistic responses consisted of students' notes taken while reading a passage and their recall protocols. High scores were to be awarded when complete information about what had been in the reading passage was present in the students' notes and recalls. Low scores were awarded when the information was incomplete, and when the students' notes and recalls contained the less important information from the passage. Results indicated strong correlations between scores awarded by human raters and those given by the computer scoring method. Equally important was the researchers' demonstration of the consistency of the scoring method with their definition of the reading–note-taking–recall process.

These few examples from second language testing begin to hint at what has been pointed out by researchers in educational measurement: that "validity research on computer-delivered and -scored constructed response examinations entails a number of considerations and complications that are less prevalent in the validation of computerized multiple-choice tests" (Williamson, Bejar & Hone, 1999). The issue is seen most clearly when the researchers detail the theoretical basis (or lack thereof) for assigning the partial scores. This detail makes it evident that a more refined definition is needed than that which is required to evaluate responses as correct or incorrect dichotomously. A right/wrong decision requires only a match of the response to the target linguistic form and therefore circumvents the useful questions of what makes the response correct, which responses are more correct than others, and on what basis the test developer would make such decisions. The more interesting and important issues begin to appear even when the test developer makes decisions about what to consider correct or incorrect (e.g., how to score misspellings), but these are magnified substantially with polytomously scored tasks.

The key to profiting from language recognition technologies in L2 testing rather than being threatened by them is to construct test tasks from which scores yield accurate and precise information relative to the construct measured. This goal requires a clear understanding of the nature of test tasks as well as clear links between construct theory and scoring method. In addition, however, as Alderson, Percsich, and Szabo (2000) pointed out, appropriate evaluation methods – not limited to correlations – need to be employed if the value of such scoring methods is to be explored. Directions for additional validation methods can be identified by consulting the standard works on validation (e.g., Messick, 1989) with particular attention to the qualitative methods of assessing strategies of test taking and rating.

Compromised security

One of the promises of CALT raised in Chapter 2 was the convenience and accessibility afforded by the Web. Roever pointed out that not only does the Web make it possible to deliver tests to learners on demand, but "the use of scoring scripts for dichotomously-scored items can make the test completely independent of the tester and increases flexibility and convenience for test takers even further" (Roever, 2001, p. 88). What increases flexibility and convenience for the test takers, however, raises concern about the validity of test scores. At the moment, this appears to be an insurmountable problem in high-stakes testing because score users need to be assured that the identity of the test taker is the same as the person for whom the score is reported. High-stakes tests such as the TOEFL cannot take advantage of this "single biggest logistical advantage" and therefore must deliver tests in testing centers, where proctors can verify the identity of the test takers. In tests used for placement and grading, the stakes are not as high, but still if such tests are left open for test takers to take "whenever it is convenient" surely score meaning is likely to be compromised and therefore scores should not be used for assigning grades and perhaps not for placement either. The validity of low-stakes tests such as DIALANG is not compromised by the logistic advantage because examinees have little or no incentive to cheat when the scores are intended only for their own information. However, low-stakes tests comprise only a small fraction of the many tests of concern to test developers and test users.

Another security issue particular to computer-adaptive testing is described by Wainer and Eignor (2000, p. 274) in their chapter entitled "Caveats, pitfalls, and unexpected consequences of implementing large-scale computerized testing." One of the pitfalls is illustrated by the story of the compromise of the computer-adaptive version of the GRE, the first large-scale testing program at Educational Testing Service to change to a computer-adaptive format. In 1994, another organization demonstrated how critical items from the item pool for that test could be easily memorized and passed on to subsequent examinees. This experience demonstrated the need for very large item pools, but it also raised awareness of the need to reconsider the security issues involved with technology, particularly when high-stakes testing is concerned. However, rather than expanding on technological methods for identity detection, futurists (e.g., Bennett, 2001) tend to point to other test uses that are lower stakes, and testing in service of the learner such as the DIALANG example. It remains to be seen whether or not the potential for Web-based low-stakes tests are realized by an array of choices of useful tests for a variety of learners.

Negative consequences

The sixth potential threat to validity of CALT stems from what may be its negative consequences or impacts on learners, language programs, and society. One type of negative consequence is evident when critics suggest that costs associated with CALT might divert money away from other program needs. Other potential negative consequences might be seen in washback on teaching if teachers focus instruction on types of tasks that appear on the test in order to prepare students to take the computer-based test. If test tasks are limited due to the constraints of the technology, as suggested above, teaching materials might be similarly limited. Such consequences have not actually been documented, and research on the washback of tests on teaching actually suggests much more complex relationships between the two types of educational events (Alderson & Hamp-Lyons, 1996), but the idea is that developers and users of CALT should be aware of the possibility of such negative consequences, and that such consequences are worthy of research.

Research on the consequences of CALT should seek to document some of the concerns that have been raised. If computer-adaptive tests are responsible for greater test anxiety than other modes of test delivery, it should be possible to document this negative impact. If examinees who know that their essay is to be scored by an automatic algorithm such as E-Rater show little interest in learning how to write and great interest in learning how computer programs score essays, it should be possible to document this interest. If intensive English students do not want to come to class, but only want to sit in the computer lab completing TOEFL-like tasks, this too could be documented through qualitative studies and survey research. This type of research would constitute evidence for negative consequences of CALT.

Along with the search for negative impact, test users should also consider the other side of the coin: the potential positive consequences of CALT. Researchers in educational measurement are exuberant about the positive potential of technology for improving assessment. Baker (1998) refers to technology as the "white horse" that arrives to save a pathetically confused and impotent system of tests and testing in US education. The technology alone cannot do it, but the key is the way that the technology supports documentation and study of better theories of knowledge, learning, and educational outcomes across the curriculum. Bennett (2001) echoes the need for educational assessment to change, in part to improve its impact on learning. In a paper analyzing the interconnectedness of assessment, technology, business, and other facets of society at an international level, he realistically points out that the scientific basis for that change is going to be second to the technology because the financial and intellectual investment that society places in technology far exceeds that which is placed in the science and art of educational assessment. "Whereas the contributions of cognitive and measurement science are in many ways more fundamental than those of new technology, it is new technology that is pervading our society" (p. 19). Bennett's perspective reformulates the concept of consequences (of tests on test users) to a more dynamic one of an interrelationship between how testing is conducted and how society is shaping the development of tools used for testing.

Conclusion

Each threat discussed in this chapter and summarized in Table 3.2 appears to be worthy of concern and research. However, based on existing research, we were not able to find any strong evidence suggesting that these threats are so insurmountable that CALT should be inherently more

Table 3.2 *Summary of potential validity threats and responses*

Potential threat to validity	Responses
Different test performance	Test users need to consider whether or not this is a real threat, and if so research is needed to compare performance on would-be parallel forms.
New task types	The interpretation of performance on new task types needs to be examined qualitatively and quantitatively so they can be used appropriately.
Limitations due to adaptive item selection	A variety of types of adaptivity needs to be explored.
Inaccurate automatic response scoring	Coordinated research and development efforts need to be directed at development of multifaceted, relevant criteria for evaluating machine scoring on a variety of constructed response items.
Compromised security	Security needs to be considered in view of the level of security required for a particular test purpose.
Negative consequences	The potential positive and negative consequences of CALT need to be understood and planned for, and then consequences need to be documented.

suspect than other types of tests. On the contrary, we noted a number of areas where additional research might be motivated by CALT, and would in turn be beneficial for language testing in general. The idea that the use of technology for assessment might actually prompt researchers to study test-taking processes more carefully might be one way that technology helps to address the complex of consequences associated with language assessment. The types of research suggested in responses to these concerns in Table 3.2 should therefore be considered as a starting point to what is necessarily a dynamic process of identifying approaches for studying issues as they arise from the needs of testers and the concerns of the public.

The general validity issues associated with CALT are the same as those for any language test: inferences and uses of test scores need to be supported by theory and research so that test users know what the scores mean and what they can be used for. At the same time, the particular threats to validity, and therefore the issues that may need to be addressed through validation research are directly related to the use of technology. A review of the existing validation research on CALT demonstrates that many important questions remain and raises questions about why so few studies have attempted to better understand the meaning of test scores from CALT, and the consequences of CALT use. Will second language testing researchers in the future take up the issues outlined in this chapter so that validity arguments about CALT can draw from a strong research base? Or will the technology-rich environment in which the next generation of test developers and test takers live change the way many of today's apparent threats to validity are viewed? In either case, developers of CALT need to be able to evaluate the extent to which any particular test is valid for its intended purpose. In Chapter 5, therefore, we will explain the issues associated with evaluation of CALT, which extend beyond examination of threats to validity. However, in order to gain insight into these issues, we turn first, in the next chapter, to a description of the resources and constraints afforded to test developers by technology.

CHAPTER FOUR

Implementing CALT

The tools required to build an assessment depend on its purpose. One can build a one-question test as a provocative start to a class without a lot of infrastructure. The teacher can develop the question based on the topic of the lecture, deliver the question orally, request the students to chose one of two responses by raising their hands, count the responses to each alternative, and remember the results. A high-stakes assessment, in contrast, requires a set of test-task specifications, a procedure for selecting particular tasks from a pool of tasks developed to these specifications, a mechanism for individual delivery of test questions, a means of individual entry of responses, a method for collating and analyzing the responses, and a means of storing results for subsequent analysis. The types of tools selected, of course, depend on the purpose of the test and a number of practical issues such as their cost, availability, and adequacy for doing the job. When the tools involve the computer for every stage of the process, the issues are still more complex. In this chapter, we describe the types of software tools that make CALT work.

It would be most satisfying to be able to describe a complete, working, sophisticated system for the development and use of CALT, but as of 2005 what we have instead are more modest systems, plans for ideal systems, and works in progress. We therefore discuss today's reality of CALT tools in this sequence. We describe the process of authoring a grammar test in a system that is relatively simplistic from the perspective of testing. Its simplicity is then revealed through our description of the design for a complex authoring system proposed to take advantage of the computer's capabilities. Next to this picture of the ideal functionality, we mention some of the ongoing efforts to develop authoring and delivery systems for language testing. This discussion of authoring tools is intended to introduce software concepts relevant to language assessment, raise issues that developers face, and present some of the current options available to test developers.

Today's authoring tools

It would be impossible to identify all of the authoring systems that might be used for authoring language assessments within computer-assisted language learning (CALL) materials. Over the past 25 years, literally dozens have appeared. They are introduced and reviewed regularly in journals such as *Language Learning & Technology, CALICO Journal,* and *ReCALL Journal.* The frequency of appearance of authoring tools attests to the fact that most developers see the value of such tools immediately upon beginning the authoring process. Many of the basic functions involved in instruction and assessment, such as presenting text and graphics on the screen and soliciting the student's response, are performed repeatedly, so it makes sense to have tools that allow the developer to author such functions as easily as possible. The number and apparent variety of such systems can be overwhelming to developers attempting to begin a CALT project. However, one needs to look at only one of these in any detail to get an idea of what comprises a basic system, and therefore we will work through the process of authoring a short grammar test in one authoring system, WebCT, only one of many possibilities, but the one that is readily available on our campus.

Authoring a test with WebCT

On our campus, like many others, if we go to the Instructional Technology Center seeking advice on developing an online grammar test for our students, the consultant will direct us without hesitation to the campus-adopted authoring and delivery system for instruction and assessment, WebCT (2004). WebCT is a tool that facilitates the creation of World Wide Web-based educational environments by users without any technical knowledge of software development. It can be used to create an entire online course, publish materials related to an existing course, and create and deliver tests. The WebCT system at Iowa State

University uses an associated program for test development, Respondus (2004), a Windows-based tool that allows users to create multiple-choice, true and false, and matching tasks, as well as short-answer and paragraph-writing tasks.

The test we will use as an example is intended for students entering our graduate applied linguistics programs. We have a requirement that all students demonstrate a certain level of metalinguistic knowledge of grammar as a prerequisite for taking an advanced grammatical analysis course. Years ago faculty therefore developed a 40-item paper-and-pencil test for this purpose. Later we wanted to create a Web-based version of the grammar test in order to make access easier for our students and grading more efficient for ourselves. We will demonstrate the authoring process by describing how the author creates the test, publishes the test on the Web, and gives students access to it. We then show what the test looks like as the student accesses it through the Web, and finally we illustrate how the records are displayed for the instructor.

Creating the test

To construct such a test, our first step is to open the Respondus program, where we are presented with the *Start* screen shown in Figure 4.1, which

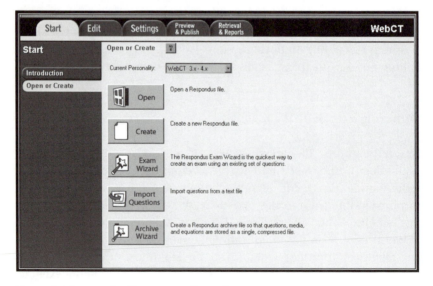

Figure 4.1 Respondus *Start* screen for authors.

has the options for opening an existing file or creating a new test. There is also an "Exam Wizard" which provides standardized templates for test creation, an option allowing the author to import questions from a file where they have been stored using another program, and an option for compressing a completed test file. In our case, we wish to create a new test, so we click on *Create*.

The *Create* button takes us to a prompt, where we are asked for a file name for the test we are creating. We name the new file "Gram Test," and then click on the *Edit* tab on the *Start* screen, which moves us to the screen shown in Figure 4.2 where we can enter the test questions and responses. Notice that we have a number of options for question types: multiple-choice, true and false, paragraph, matching, short-answer, and multiple-response. In developing the paper-and-pencil version of this test, the faculty had decided that a multiple-choice question type was appropriate for testing the level of metalinguistic knowledge of interest, so in WebCT, we selected that option, which results in a multiple-choice frame displayed with prompts for entering the relevant information.

As shown in Figure 4.2, this *Edit* screen allows us to give the question an identifier, enter the question text and the answer choices, indicate the

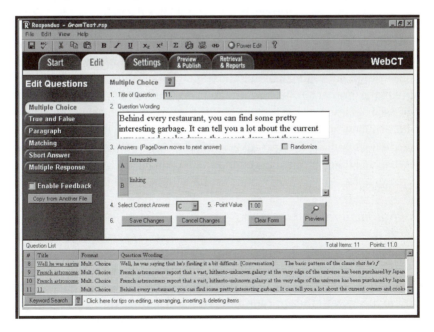

Figure 4.2 Respondus *Edit* screen for authors.

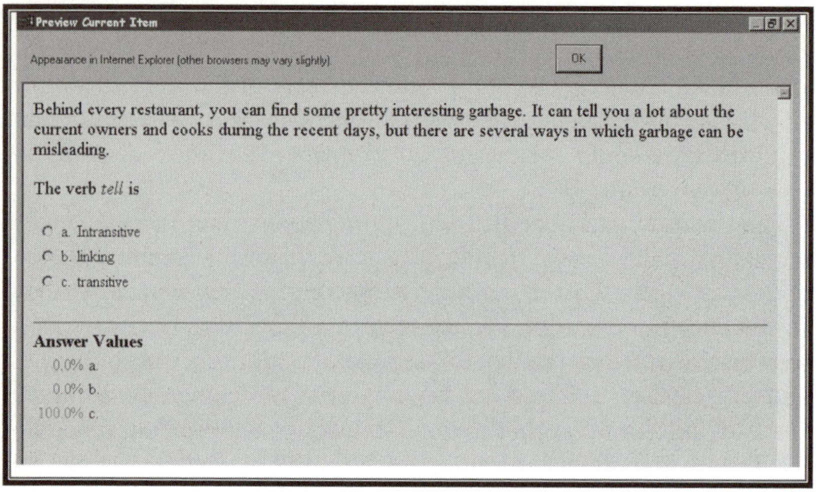

Figure 4.3 Respondus New Test Task Preview for authors.

correct answer and the number of points it is to receive, and then click on the *Save* button. The *Preview & Publish* tab on this screen allows the author to look at how the question will appear for the student in its finished form one question at a time without actually publishing it. Figure 4.3 shows how the question appears on this preview screen for the author.

When all the questions have been entered and saved, we are ready to move to the *Settings* screen, which gives us a number of options for test presentation, including whether the test takers see the entire test at once or one question at a time, and whether they can revisit previous tasks or not. Settings also include how and when the scores are released to the test takers and what information they are given, such as the text for each question as well as the test taker's answer, and whether the test taker receives feedback in the form of an explanation for each correct option.

Publishing the test on the Web

The next step in the Respondus test creation process is the *Preview & Publish* screen. When the test file is complete and correct, we are ready to designate a WebCT server where the test is to be located. Local systems prompt users with the appropriate server and add the questions to a test database for incorporation into other tests later as well as the current test. The *Publish* screen is shown in Figure 4.4.

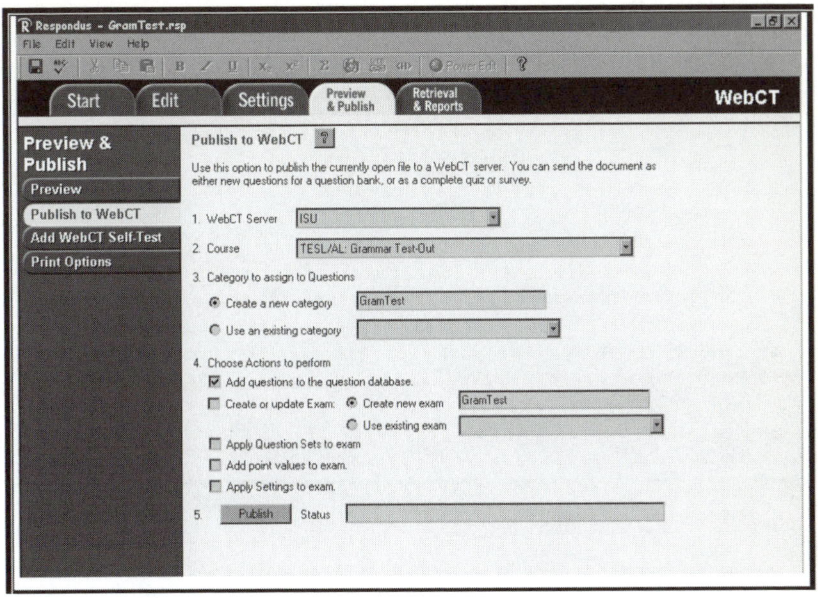

Figure 4.4 Respondus *Preview & Publish* screen for authors.

When we click the *Publish* button, Respondus uploads the file from the local computer to the server, where it will be available for incorporation into WebCT and available for our students to access. We are not quite finished with Respondus, however. The Respondus *Retrieval and Reports* screen gives us a number of options for how the test results are reported, including receiving summary statistics for groups of test takers, and how many test takers chose each answer option.

Giving students access to the test

We are now ready to log on to WebCT to make the test available to our students. At this stage, we can add the test instructions, modify the page colors, and add icons, as shown in Figure 4.5.

WebCT also provides a *Control Panel* with a number of options, including making the test available to test takers. We also need to tell WebCT which students may log on to take the test, a task that is also handled from the *Control Panel*. Finally, we can preview the test to make certain it appears the way we want it to and will be easily accessible for our test

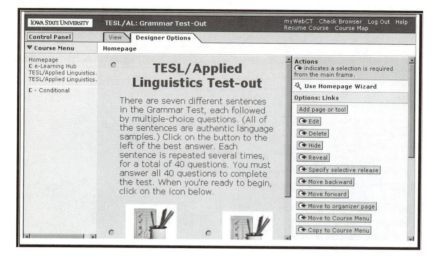

Figure 4.5 WebCT Designer Page for authors.

takers. If we identify problems or errors in what we have entered, we would return to the *Edit* screen to make changes. If we do not want to make changes, the test is now ready for our test takers.

Taking the test

When the test taker logs on to WebCT to take the test, he or she is sent to the homepage we designed, containing the instructions, as shown in Figure 4.6.

When the icon is clicked, the test taker is given a set of generic instructions from WebCT, as shown in Figure 4.7. These instructions tell test takers how to begin the test, how the questions will be presented, what to expect to see on the screen, how to answer the questions, and what to do if technical problems arise such as browser or computer crashes. When the test takers click the *Begin* button, the test is presented in the format we selected on the *Settings* screen in Respondus, in this case one question at a time, as shown in Figure 4.8.

Notice that the screen shows the test taker's name, the date, and the number of questions in the test. A button allows the test taker to save the answer and another one lets her move to the next question. The frame on the right indicates which questions the test taker has answered and saved. Finally, the *Finish* button submits the test for scoring.

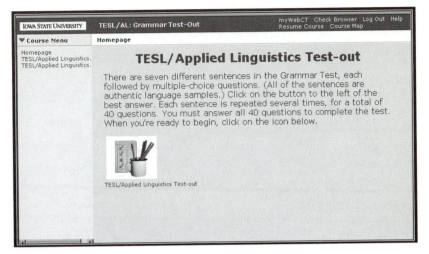

Figure 4.6 WebCT Test Homepage as seen by test takers.

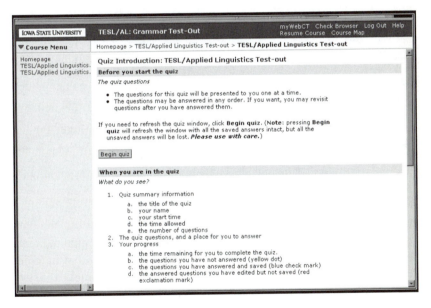

Figure 4.7 Generic WebCT instructions for test takers.

Viewing examinees' records

WebCT stores the records of examinees on the test and allows instructors to see each test taker's score on the test as well as review the test taker's performance on each question, as shown in Figure 4.9. In this example,

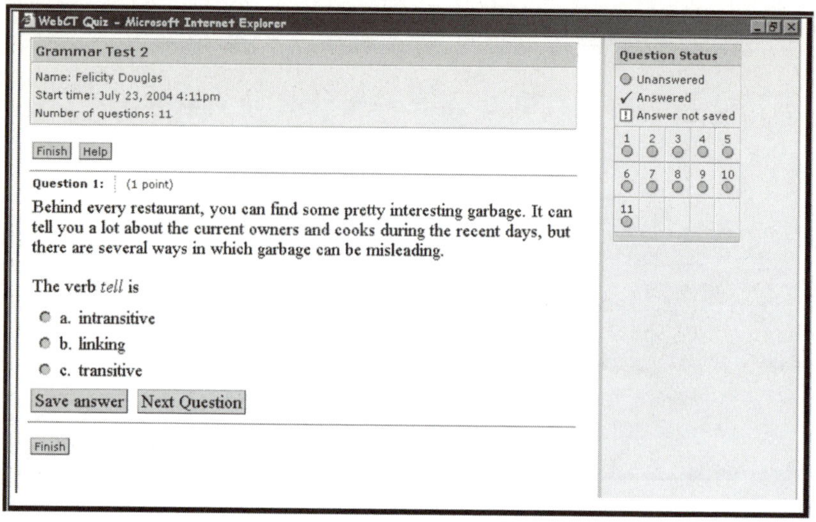

Figure 4.8 WebCT question presentation screen as seen by test takers.

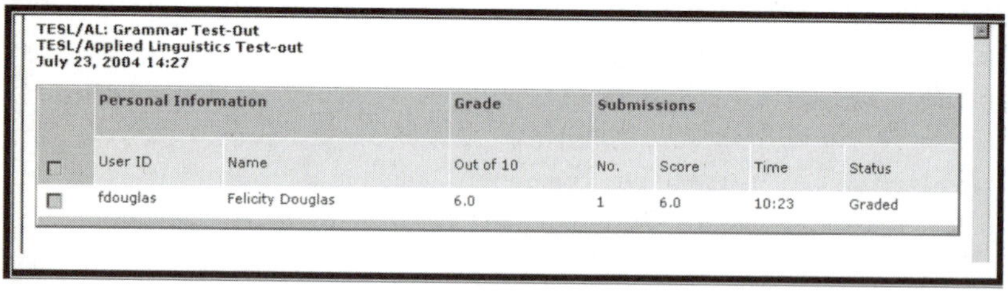

Figure 4.9 WebCT individual test taker report.

Felicity Douglas was the only test taker, but when the test is actually used by more students each score will appear in this record folder.

We can also retrieve a summary of responses on each question, i.e., a classical item analysis, when the entire group of test takers has completed the test, from the database that the program sets up, with options that we can select. The report includes the percentage of the test takers who got the question correct, the percentages of the top and bottom 25% who got it correct, and the discrimination index (calculated as the difference in performance between the top and bottom groups).

WebCT helped immensely in allowing us to transform a selected-response test into an online test that students can take at their time and place of convenience. WebCT matches examinees' responses with the

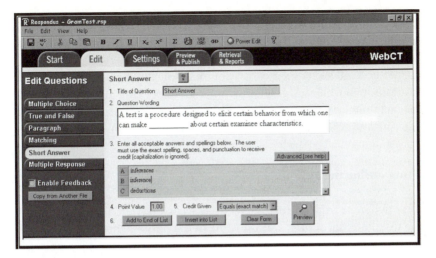

Figure 4.10 Respondus Short-Answer *Edit* page for authors.

ones we specified as correct, totals the score, and places it in a database, where the instructor can view it later. In our setting, WebCT/Respondus is convenient and easy to use, and provides a fairly wide range of types of test tasks, including multiple-choice with single or multiple correct responses, true and false, paragraph writing from a prompt, matching items in two columns, short-answer with automatic scoring, and question sets based on written or aural input. For example, the short-answer option allows the test developer to construct a blank-filling task and designate multiple acceptable answers, as shown in Figure 4.10.

Both "inferences" and the singular "inference" have been entered as acceptable responses, as has the synonym "deductions." Should a test taker respond with another close synonym, such as "judgments", it would be counted as incorrect, unless the test developer had designated it as an acceptable option during the design stage. If a test taker should misspell the response or make a typo, this too would be counted as incorrect, again unless the developer could foresee all possible permutations of acceptable responses and enter these into the list.

In addition to the selected response tasks, the paragraph option on the *Edit* page provides for an extended-response task, an essay from 5 to 100 lines long, which must be rated manually. These examples illustrate that WebCT/Respondus provides the test developer with a degree of flexibility in the types of tasks that can be created for a Web-based language test. However, WebCT's tools are necessarily general-purpose ones which can be used for developing assessments for engineering, and political science as well as metalinguistic grammatical knowledge. With respect to testing languages other than English, our colleagues working with non-Roman characters find WebCT's mechanism for displaying these unacceptable. In addition, the clearest limitation for testing speaking in any language is the fact that the current version does not give the developer the option of eliciting and capturing spoken responses from the examinee.

Other authoring systems

Although our campus provides licensed access to WebCT for members of the instructional staff, it was only one of the options that we could have chosen. One well-known free-access set of test authoring tools for language teaching and assessment is Hot Potatoes (Half-baked, 2004), a downloadable suite of six programs that enable the test developer to create standard test-task formats: multiple-choice, short-answer, jumbled-sentence, crossword, matching/ordering and gap-filling. The test creation procedure is very transparent (easier than Repondus, for example) and the result is a fairly simple format, shown in Figure 4.11 below, that can include a graphic and a link to another page (a reading passage, for example). The finished test can be mounted on the instructor's website or on the Half-baked site.

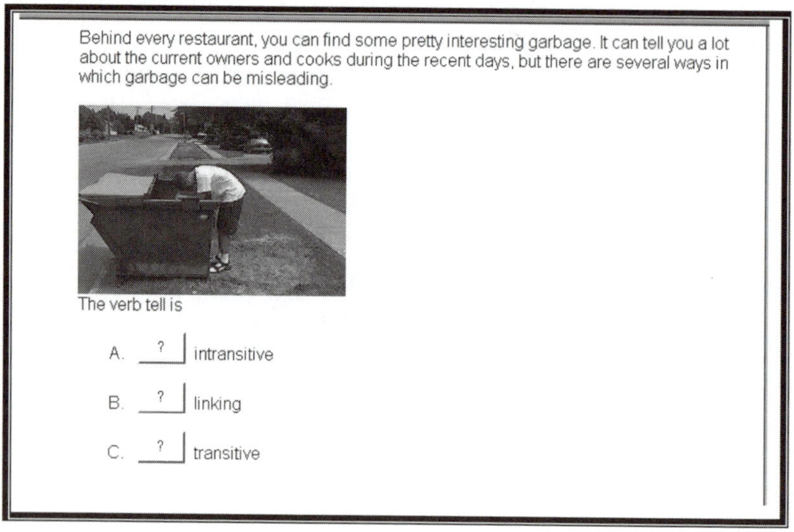

Figure 4.11 Sample Hot Potatoes test.

A similarly easy-to-use tool is the Discovery School Quiz Center (Discovery School, 2004). After becoming a member of Custom Classroom at the Discovery School website (which is free of charge), the test developer can make short-answer, true and false, multiple-choice, and essay tasks, or tasks which combine these formats. The resulting test, as shown in Figure 4.12 below, is mounted on the Discovery website under the author's name where it can be accessed by test takers. Scores and feedback are sent by email to the instructor and to the test taker.

Examples of more sophisticated authoring tools, similar in features to WebCT/Respondus, are Blackboard (2004) and Questionmark (2004). Also like WebCT, these systems are licensed (i.e., not free) products that offer a range of features and user support, including a variety of response procedures such as hot spot, and drag and drop, as well as allowing for use of sound, video, Java, and Macromedia Flash in creating test tasks. Blackboard and Questionmark offer the test developer an array of test formats similar to that offered by the other authoring systems we have discussed: multiple-choice, essay, gap-filling, and matching/ranking. What they all lack is flexibility in some areas where the developer of the authoring system has made decisions that may not harmonize with the wishes of the test developer. Because of the basic technical similarities among these systems, most users, like us, choose their authoring tools on the basis of what is readily available in terms of cost, logistics, and support. For those working with non-Roman fonts, how the system handles these characters becomes the most critical factor.

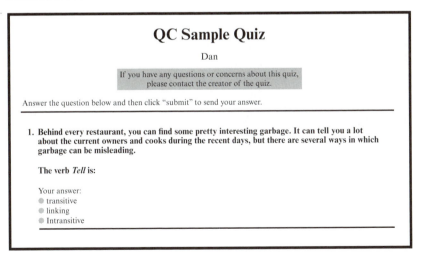

Figure 4.12 Quiz Center sample task.

Systems underlying assessment

Many testing specialists would see existing published authoring tools as overly simplistic relative to the needs of assessment. Suggestions for more sophisticated systems include the need for functionality such as the following: estimation of task difficulty, analysis of learners' language, creating and organizing objects to be used in constructing tests and instruction, a means for gathering process data, a structure for collecting relevant data in a learner model (Chapelle, 2001, pp. 170–5). Describing a system with many of these functionalities, Almond, Steinberg, and Mislevy (2002) point out that if developers are to have access to these types of complex processes, it is necessary "to create a common framework of design architecture that enables the delivery of operational assessments that can be easily adapted to meet multiple purposes" (p. 3). Their description of such an architecture depicts an assessment system which contains the processes and structures that are needed to provide the rich functionality that one would hope for in CALT, because it provides for not only test development and delivery, but also research. Even though this system is a plan rather than an operational system, it provides an informative backdrop for examining the authoring tools currently available for language assessment.

The basic principle underlying Almond, Steinberg and Mislevy's four-process architecture is the need for a system that contains the processes and structures routinely used in assessment to be constructed in a way that they can be appropriately modified and used repeatedly for a wide variety of assessments, including language testing. Moreover, it is to support the full range of test purposes from low-stakes classroom assessments, to high-stakes tests. They identify the parameters of the various tests as follows: "Each purpose for which the product will be used defines a particular requirement for the security of the tasks, the reliability of the results, the nature and timing of the feedback, and the level of detail of the reported [results]" (Almond, Steinberg & Mislevy, 2002). The architecture that they propose to account for these needs is depicted in Figure 4.13 and described below.

The four processes in the system rely on a database shown in the center of the figure which holds test tasks and other data that may be needed for some test uses, such as a record of the examinee's estimated ability level so far in the testing process during test taking. The combination of the

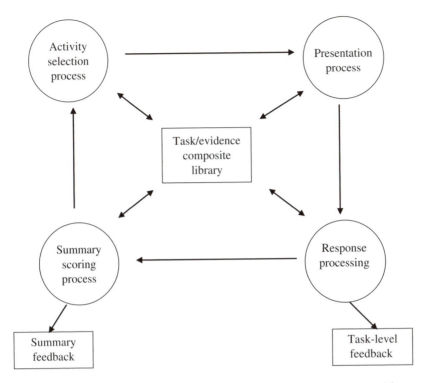

Figure 4.13 A four-process architecture for an assessment system (adapted from Almond, Steinberg & Mislevy, 2002, p. 7).

four processes produces two types of data as output, one of which is the "summary feedback," typically a test score. The other is the "task-level feedback," which can be requested for some test uses such as a low-stakes assessment, in which a total score would be less informative than specific information about correctness during test taking.

Activity selection process

The *activity selection process* is the means by which particular tasks are chosen for a test. In the WebCT authoring process described above, the test was entered by the author and then presented as such to each test taker in a predetermined fashion. Almond, Steinberg, and Mislevy's architecture would make activity selection a dynamic process whereby the computer would select activities from the database on the basis of factors such as the content of the activity, the status of the evidence model (i.e., information about the test taker's ability) during test taking, the reliability of the score required, or concerns for security. The author would consider these factors to determine how to set the parameters of the activity selection process.

The presentation process

The *presentation process* is the most transparent to test takers and observers because it is the process by which the instructions, input, and prompts are displayed on the screen or transmitted through audio or video. In the WebCT test, many of the decisions about the instructions and presentation were set automatically when we selected multiple-choice as the type of activity. Presentation of other character fonts or alternative presentations would have presented a challenge, as would eliciting oral language or text using different fonts. Almond, Steinberg, and Mislevy's architecture would provide a means for modifying these aspects of presentation by leaving decisions about instructions and input to the test taker, and expected responses open for the author to define.

Response processing

Response processing refers to the evaluation of each of the examinee's responses. In language assessment, this process is particularly complex and important because for many testing purposes the linguistic detail of the examinee's constructed responses needs to be scored precisely. WebCT included two item formats that allowed for written constructed responses, the short-answer and the paragraph responses; however, neither of these types was to be scored through linguistic analysis of the response. Almond, Steinberg, and Mislevy's architecture would presumably allow for such subsystems of analysis. It would also provide a means for the author to specify when and what kind of feedback the test taker would receive during test taking. Feedback could therefore consist of mark-up on spelling and grammar as well as on overall correctness. Moreover, the specific performance data would be added to the "evidence model" in the database during test taking for use by the other systems, such as activity selection. Thus the response scoring is one aspect of the procedure that allows for item-level adaptivity. In this architecture, the adaptivity could in principle be based on any aspect of the test taker's performance rather than the familiar adaptivity based on responses to multiple-choice items.

Summary scoring process

The *summary scoring process* collects the individual response scores and combines them in a manner specified by the author to produce a total score or other type of report. In the WebCT example, the score is the result of the scores added for all of the test items, as specified by the weights given by the author. Almond, Steinberg, and Mislevy's architecture would offer flexibility in creating scores in a variety of ways such as diagnostic scores comprised of information from different components of the tasks or item difficulties of items answered correctly.

It is not fair to compare dynamic systems such as WebCT, which authors use on a daily basis to construct tests, to static plans on the drawing table. At the same time, it is useful to look beyond the inflexibility that some authors would associate with computer-based tests to the real potentials of technology. In Almond, Steinberg, and Mislevy's plan, the database containing test tasks and evidence about the test taker is key to the flexibility of the system because it holds information in a form that allows authors to specify a wide range of options for test delivery and scoring. Some of these ideas are put into place in some of the authoring tools being developed today.

Under construction in 2005

Some testing practitioners are engaged in developing their own authoring software in order to achieve greater control over desired options. For example, the developers of the WebLAS system at UCLA (UCLA, 2001) wanted to develop a system that would allow them to construct web-based assessments in three languages (English, Japanese, and Korean) for placing up to 1,700 university students in appropriate language classes, diagnose areas of strength and weakness, and monitor progress. They developed an authoring system with the following components:

These components correspond to those discussed in the section above:

1. Task development system

   user-friendly for content specialists (classroom teachers); tasks easily integrated into task bank

2. Task delivery system

   attractively designed, engaging web-based assessment tasks, linked to database and potentially automated assembly algorithm

3. Data management system

   automated capture, scoring, data processing, analysis, reporting, storage and retrieval of assessment results

(UCLA Applied Linguistics and Center for Digital Humanities 2001–2003)

activity selection process (UCLA Task Development System), presentation process (UCLA Task Delivery System), and response processing and summary scoring processes (UCLA Data Management System). The resulting set of tools has allowed for development of three general types of language assessment tasks (listening, reading, and writing), using multimedia input and response (text, graphics, audio, video), in three different languages with differing orthographies. The features of WebLAS therefore allow authors to construct tests that would be difficult to produce without the authoring tools.

This example of an "in-house" test authoring system illustrates the fact that educational and testing programs developing medium- to high-stakes tests find it worthwhile to develop their own authoring systems in order to achieve flexibility in specifying the full range of components and features rather than employing an "off-the-shelf" product, whether commercial or freeware. In addition to the WebLAS project larger programs that we discussed in Chapter 2, such as DIALANG and TOEFL, followed this path, as well, and with substantial costs incurred. The development of proprietary software for test authoring requires a team that includes members with complementary expertise in assessment, human factors, programming and management, as well as the financial resources usually only available to large programs. Another alternative to using ready-made templates or developing one's own authoring system which we will just mention here is to approach commercial test development companies that will work with clients to create the types of tests the client specifies. This can also be an expensive option, of course. Examples of such companies include Promissor, inc. (Promissor, 2004) and Enlight AB (Enlight, 2004).

Conclusion

The ideal tools required for test development depend on the purpose of the assessment and practical issues such as the resources of time, money, and expertise to be allocated to assessment. WebCT worked well for our grammar test, but if we had wanted to make the test adaptive, or require spoken responses from the examinees, for example, we would have needed to look beyond the recommendation of our Instructional Technology Center. Beyond the example test we illustrated, however, it is also essential to consider the scope of options that technology may offer for authors of language tests in the future. This forward look should prove informative to the many testing researchers and test developers who have found the need to design their own authoring tools. Complex questions about the trade-offs involved in adopting or developing authoring tools might ultimately be informed by methods for evaluating the tests that result from their use. In the following chapter, we examine the issues involved in the evaluation of CALT.

CHAPTER FIVE

Evaluating CALT

If CALT is different from other forms of testing, should computer-based testing be evaluated against a different set of standards from that used to evaluate other tests? Chapter 3 focused specifically on the potential threats that may limit the validity of inferences and uses of CALT. Such threats have occupied the public's attention, but this chapter takes up the more technical issue of how CALT should be evaluated overall. Surely, an evaluation of the quality of a test should not be centered entirely on the aspects of the test that catch the attention of the informed layperson. This chapter addresses CALT evaluation in view of specific suggestions that have been made by CALT developers. These suggestions in particular and CALT evaluation more generally are discussed from the perspective of the profession's views of how all language tests should be evaluated. It begins with a look at guidelines and advice suggested to promote quality during CALT development and evaluation, and then summarizes research focused on specific aspects of CALT quality. A subsequent section demonstrates the types of findings obtained through the use of Bachman and Palmer's (1996) test usefulness framework. The final part discusses CALT evaluation within more recent perspectives in educational measurement (Kane, 2001) about developing a validity argument through the definition of inferences intended to underlie score interpretation and use. We argue that specific technology-related issues should be placed within a broader framework of test evaluation.

Guidelines and advice

From the time that computer-assisted testing began to be established in the 1970s, the unique set of issues posed by the medium was recognized by educational measurement researchers. In 1984, "Technical guidelines for assessing computer-adaptive tests," by Green, Bock, Humphreys, Linn, and Reckase, was published in the *Journal of Educational Measurement*, and five years later the American Psychological Association had published *Guidelines for Computer-Based Tests and Interpretations*. These publications along with Green's (1988) "Construct validity of computer-based tests," in the seminal volume *Test Validity*, and Baker's (1989) "Computer technology in test construction and processing," in the authoritative third edition of *Educational Measurement*, forecasted the pervasive sense within the educational measurement profession that evaluation of computer-assisted tests should be undertaken differently or with a different set of criteria from the evaluation of other tests.

This perspective from educational measurement has been evident in language assessment to some extent. Noijons (1994) suggested a set of test factors that should be considered in the evaluation of CALT. These factors appear to be intended as an addition to the requirements of validity and reliability that Noijons treats in a separate part of the paper. He draws on the criteria for evaluating computer-assisted testing suggested by Alessi and Trollop (1985), authors of a well-respected text on computer-assisted instruction. This conceptualization distinguishes between two types of factors, those pertaining to test content, and those associated with test taking, as summarized in Table 5.1.

Some unique characteristics of CALT are evident in the points raised by Noijons, for example providing examinees with information about the online help available, providing feedback when inappropriate functions are chosen, giving an indication of when the test is finished, terminating the test without losing the examinee's responses, in case of equipment/ software breakdown, and securely storing data. These aspects of interface design add an additional layer of factors to those that are typically considered by evaluators when identifying factors that might negatively affect the test-taking process (and therefore test scores) if they are not appropriately addressed. Other factors such as the feedback that the examinees receive, whether or not the test is speeded, and how results are to be presented to examinees are issues that pertain to all language tests, but in CALT the number of options is dramatically increased. For example, on a paper-and-pencil test, the options for feedback to examinees consist of providing

Table 5.1 *Summary of points for evaluation of CALT outlined by Noijons (1994)*

Timing	Test content	Taking the test
Before	Function/purpose of test: What is the educational objective? (mastery, placement, classification, selection) Test objective: What does the test intend to assess?	Entrance to test: What data are registered? (candidate's ID, test number, candidate's responses) Test instructions: What is the candidate told? (procedures for test taking, what is tested, what help is available online)
	Test length: How many items are on the test?	Examples of items: What examples of items are available? Do the examinees have an opportunity to try out responding and indicate that they understand how to respond?
	Generating items: How are items selected from an item bank?	Check of the test: Has the test been checked over by developers and by other experts?
During	Item type: What is the format for responses?	Fraud: Can the test be terminated without losing examinees' responses in case he or she is found to be cheating?
	Feedback: What messages do the examinees receive about test-taking procedures or about the content of their performance? Time: Is the test speeded?	Breakdowns: Are procedures in place in case of equipment or software breakdowns? (saving data, instructions for examinees) Feedback: Is there feedback to the examinees when they perform functions that are not permitted?
	Registration of responses: How are responses obtained and stored?	End of test: Is the candidate informed about the amount of time remaining if the test is timed? Are there instructions about what to do at the end of the test?
After	Evaluation: How is a decision made based on test results?	Storage of data: Are the data protected in a way that the examinees cannot access them?
	Presentation of test results: How are results presented to examinees?	Printing of data: Are data printed as a measure to back up the information?

information on correctness of responses through total and part scores, after the test has been completed. On a computer-based test, in contrast, we have discussed a number of options in earlier chapters for providing feedback during test taking, as well as detailed immediate feedback at the end of the test. The test developer needs to explicitly choose how feedback is integrated into the test-taking process, and the evaluator needs to consider the appropriateness of the choices.

Many of the unique CALT concerns evident in Noijons' analysis fall within the domain of interface issues as described by Fulcher (2003), who takes the perspective of the test developer and therefore outlines the interface issues to be taken into account during the process of developing CALT. He divides the issues into three phases, (1) planning and initial design, (2) usability testing, and then (3) field trials and fine tuning. Table 5.2 summarizes the considerations to be addressed by test developers in the first phase. These include advice on the factors that beginning developers in particular find overwhelming. As Chapter 4 showed, developers typically work with authoring systems that would allow the author to specify some of these (e.g., selecting item types), but would provide pre-specified forms for others (e.g., reserved words and symbols for control of the interface).

Although Fulcher's analysis is not framed as an evaluation, the advice to the designers implies points around which evaluation would presumably be conducted. The evaluative impetus is evident in the way Fulcher describes his purpose in specifying the guidelines: to work toward development of a "computer interface that does not interfere with assessment." The imperative is that the mode of test delivery should "not contaminate scores, thus threatening valid interpretation" (p. 387). The idea is to make the interface invisible because any contribution of the interface to test scores would negatively affect the interpretation of test scores as an indication of language ability. As we pointed out in the previous chapter, however, the extent to which the interface should be invisible for a particular test depends on whether it threatens to act as an unmotivated source of variance in performance, which in turn depends on what is to be measured.

Table 5.3 summarizes Fulcher's Phase II and III activities, which consist of processes that are normally included in large-scale test development, such as item writing and banking, in addition to many that are specific to development of CALT, such as searching for problems and solutions in the interface, verifying that it works across sites and platforms, and seeking interface-related sources of variance. Like Phase I activities, these

Table 5.2 *Considerations for Phase I of the process in designing an interface for a computer-based language test (summarized from Fulcher, 2003)*

Category of design issue	General considerations and processes	Points of concern and advice for designers
1. Designing prototypes	Hardware considerations	Computer specifications, screen resolution, download time
	Software considerations	Browser compatibility, third-party software, authoring software
2. Good interface design	Navigation	Navigation buttons and icons; operating system buttons and instructions; ease and speed of navigation; clarity of page titles; explicit decisions about revisiting pages during test taking; safety measure to minimize mis-navigation
	Terminology	Establish reserved words for interface flow
	Page layout	Avoid overcrowding with text, minimize scrolling, avoid upper case
	Text	Avoid complex, distracting animation; use a font size larger than 10 point; make explicit decisions about whether examinees should be able to alter the font size, use a familiar font, avoid mixing fonts
	Text color	Maximize contrast among colors if color is significant (e.g., instructions vs. reading passage)
	Toolbars and controls	Present as few options as possible and place the most important information first
	Icons and graphics	Minimize the number of icons used; optimize size for visual appearance and download time; avoid animated and blinking images; display icons to update test taker during delays
	Help facilities	Make explicit decisions about the availability of help
	Outside the test	Consider use of outside sources to assess a particular construct
	Item types	Optimize the number of types needed in view of the construct and the test taker's capacity to change types

Table 5.2 *(continued)*

Category of design issue	General considerations and processes	Points of concern and advice for designers
	Multimedia	Ensure consistent presentation and efficient download time
	Forms for writing and short-answer tasks	Leave enough space for the response; align and justify multiple text boxes; arrange multiple boxes vertically
	Feedback	Type, timing and location of feedback should be planned
3. Concurrent Phase I activities	Development of delivery systems; investigation of score retrieval and database storage; distribution and retrieval for sections scored by human raters; scoring algorithms and rubrics; familiarity studies; technology studies; construct-validity studies; small-scale trialing	(Specific advice on these general areas is beyond the scope of Fulcher's paper.)

Table 5.3 *Considerations for Phase II and Phase III of the process in designing an interface for a computer-based language test (summarized from Fulcher, 2003)*

Phase	Category of design issue
II. Usability testing	1. Searching for problems and solutions
	2. Selecting test takers for usability studies
	3. Concurrent activities: item writing and banking; pre-testing; trialing score rubrics; constructing structural construct studies
III. Field testing and fine tuning	1. Verifying that the interface works across sites and platforms
	2. Seeking interface-related sources of variance
	3. Concurrent activities: developing tutorials, producing practice/example tests; developing rater training packages and conducting rater training; considering scaling studies and score reporting; planning further validation studies

are listed as recommended processes, with the implication that evaluation of the completed test would include evaluation of the extent to which these steps had been taken.

A more global approach to evaluation identifies desirable features that CALT should have, based on the capabilities of technology and the perceived needs in language testing. Meunier (1994) takes such an approach in a paper enumerating advantages and disadvantages of computer-adaptive testing (CAT). After identifying "questionable construct validity" as one disadvantage, she draws on five validity-related qualities for an evaluation of the validity of CAT: content validity, concurrent validity, predictive validity, construct validity, face validity, as well as test bias. In discussing these she mentions research methods for investigating them and actual research conducted on CAT. The outcome from Meunier's discussion of evaluation is to propose "to replace multiple-choice and cloze formats, and to apply the potential of CALT to live-action simulations . . .[to] assess students with respect to their ability to function in situations with various levels of difficulty" (Meunier, 1994, p. 37). Laurier's (2000) analysis points in the same direction: the capabilities of the computer make it possible to construct tests with positive qualities such as authenticity, which he focuses on. These two papers focus on the ideal – what could be – in order to challenge future test developers.

Although both the detailed guidelines and the broad advice point to features that have been or should be given particular attention by developers and users of CALT, they do not describe empirical means of investigating CALT or even direct researchers to the relevant empirical questions. Such questions and methods, however, are apparent in some of the research that has investigated particular computer-based tests, which we address next.

Evaluative research on CALT

In Chapter 3 we discussed some of the research intended to address threats to validity. This approach to CALT focuses on what might be wrong with the scores obtained from CALT. Despite the variety of concerns outlined in Chapter 3, the most consistent research theme associated with CALT is the investigation of the quality and efficiency of computer-adaptive tests. Other themes such as the quality of computer-assisted response scoring and the impact of CALT on learners' affect and performance have been addressed to a lesser extent.

Quality and efficiency

Studies reporting on the development and evaluation of computer-adaptive language tests discuss issues raised by the need for independent items (e.g., Kaya-Carton, Carton & Dandonoli, 1991), correlations with other tests (e.g., Stevenson & Gross, 1991), and the fit of the examinees' responses to an IRT model. However, the unifying theme of studies of computer-adaptive tests reflects what Chalhoub-Deville refers to as "perhaps the greatest attraction of CAT": the potential for administering large scale tests in a way that optimizes "the testing situation by targeting each student's ability level" (1999, p. ix). Key data in such contexts are therefore records of the actual amount of time that each examinee spent taking the test, the psychometric model that was used to obtain the results, and the reliability of the results. The papers in Chalhoub-Deville's (1999) edited volume that discuss test development (e.g., Dunkel, 1999; Laurier, 1999) provide examples of the complex issues that arise in working through the decisions developers must make about test purpose, test content, psychometric models, software, and hardware. Other papers focus on issues of psychometric model selection (Blais & Laurier, 1993), model fit for examinees with different first languages (Brown & Iwashita, 1996) and other operational issues (Burston & Monville-Burston, 1995; Young, Shermis, Brutten & Perkins, 1996).

Evaluation of linguistic responses

In Chapter 3, machine evaluation of linguistic responses was discussed in terms of minimizing threats to construct validity, but the early work in this area points to some other issues. Molholt and Presler (1986) introduced their pilot study of machine rating of oral test responses with two motivations for exploring such techniques:

1. Machine rating is much more efficient than human rating, especially when dealing with large amounts of data.
2. Machine rating could be used to identify and classify weak areas of pronunciation as part of a system of computer-assisted instruction in pronunciation. (p. 113)

They set out to evaluate the quality of the computational analysis of 20 ESL examinees on the reading aloud passage, which was one task on the Test of Spoken English (Educational Testing Service, 1986) at the time of the research. The computer-derived scores were calculated by matching the fundamental frequency analysis of the examinees' spoken test responses against that of the model template and marking errors and deviations, which included missing phonemes, wrong phonemes, partial phonemes, extra phonemes, and improper stress. The analysis consisted of a Spearman rho correlation coefficient (.93) between the scores produced by the human raters and those calculated by machine. Other studies of linguistic analysis of responses did not always result in such positive findings (e.g., Reid, 1986), but as suggested in Chapter 3, the larger issue seems to be the need for other means of assessing the value of linguistic analysis that are more informative than correlations of total scores with a criterion.

The second goal that Molholt and Presler (1986) laid out requires a more delicate analysis than a correlation between holistic human and machine ratings. Such analyses are needed to step toward the ultimate goal of qualitatively changing assessment practices in ways that could benefit learners. The goal of using linguistic analysis for diagnosis means that the computer will surpass what can be accomplished routinely by human raters, and therefore a research methodology seeking only to match what human raters do is not appropriate. These issues have been explored in educational measurement for some time (e.g., Birenbaum & Tatsuoka, 1987; Mislevy, 1993), but not in language assessment.

Impact on affect, performance, and efficiency

Research concerned with investigating relative benefits and detriments of operational CALT documents the efficiency of CALT relative to paper-and-pencil testing and its effects on examinees. The large-scale computer familiarity study of the TOEFL program in the mid-1990s was one such example discussed in Chapter 3, but ten years earlier at Brigham Young University similar issues were investigated when one of the first computer-adaptive ESL tests was operationalized (Madsen, 1986). After a trial event in December 1985, a computer-adaptive placement test for reading and grammar with a 300-item bank was administered to 42 ESL students. Data were collected about examinees' demographic information and the time they took to complete each segment of the test in addition to responses on a Likert scale to questions about the following:

- Previous computer experience
- Emotive reactions prior to the test

- Emotive reactions following the test
- Relative difficulty of the two tests
- Clarity of the instructions
- Evaluation of the length of the test
- Clarity of the computer screen   (Madsen, 1986, p. 43)

In addition, examinees were asked to complete open-ended questions concerning what, if anything, they liked and did not like about the test. Although some differences were found between speakers of different L1s, the overall conclusion was that "micro-computer programs utilizing the one-parameter Rasch model hold out the promise of providing accurate adaptive or tailored tests that are less stressful for most students as well as more efficient measures." This study and the TOEFL study, which were conceived over 20 and 10 years ago, respectively, would need to be reconceptualized today in view of the fact that many examinees are accustomed to working with technology, but they demonstrate methodologies for test evaluation that take into account potential influences of technology in the testing process.

Summary

Past research on CALT has focused on the primary concerns of the test developers, and therefore each individual study tells only part of the story of the evaluation of CALT. Much like the approach taken in Chapter 3, each study has been directed toward what were seen as specific threats, potential problems, or intended benefits of CALT in a particular testing situation. As a consequence, the large majority of research on CALT has addressed familiar matters such as model fit of the data and the impact of CALT on examinees. These issues, along with those discussed in Chapter 3, constitute the canonical research on validity and reliability, if we consider validity in the broad sense as pertaining to the interpretation of test scores and the consequences of test use. In language testing, however, the goal has been to identify these along with other desirable qualities and to integrate evidence about all of these into an argument about the usefulness of a test for a particular purpose. Moreover, as many of the points raised by Fulcher suggest, the evaluation of a test should not be limited to empirical research conducted after the test has been completed and is being used.

Justifying overall usefulness

CALT evaluation is presented by Chapelle (2001) within a more comprehensive scheme for evaluation of test usefulness (Bachman & Palmer, 1996), which lays out six criteria intended to guide evaluation of any particular assessment: reliability, construct validity, authenticity, interactiveness, impact, and practicality. These ideal qualities can be evaluated on the basis of judgmental opinion and empirical data; examples of this process are given in Bachman and Palmer's book, and CALT evaluation within this framework has been illustrated for several computer-based language tests (Chapelle, 2001; Chapelle, Jamieson & Hegelheimer, 2003). The aim is to have a means of evaluating CALT which is consistent with established practices in the field rather than being controlled by a separate and unequal set of concerns. By applying the usefulness analysis to four computer-assisted assessments, Chapelle (2001) identified some of the positive and negative features associated with the technology and pertaining to the concerns of language assessment. Table 5.4, contains a summary of such analyses which builds on the one summarized by Chapelle (2001).

These positive and negative factors are based on an analysis of four tests. One was a computer-adaptive reading test concerned with making inferences about learners' ESL reading comprehension to be used for decisions about placement into an intensive ESL program (Madsen, 1991). The second was an ESL listening test investigated by the TOEFL program during its exploration of computer-assisted TOEFL (Taylor, Kirsch, Eignor & Jamieson, 1999). The third was a writing test for native speakers of English investigated in a pilot project by Powers, Fowles, Farnum, and Ramsey (1994). The fourth was from a research project investigating a response analysis program for recognition of test takers' linguistic responses on an ESL reading test (Henning, Anbar, Helm & D'Arcy, 1993). In addition to observations drawn from those four tests, however, further points have been added to this summary on the basis of our experience in working with computer-based tests.

Reliability

The first positive quality for reliability came from the analysis of the reading test with open-ended questions requiring the examinee to construct a response. When such a response is incorrect, it may be partially

Table 5.4 *Technology-related positive and negative aspects of CALT (adapted from Chapelle, 2001, p. 115)*

Quality	Positive attributes	Negative attributes
Reliability	Partial-credit scoring implemented by computer should provide more precise measurement, larger variance in scores, and high coefficient-alpha reliabilities. Computer-assisted scoring rubrics perform consistently from one occasion to another. CAT algorithms test continuously until a score with the desired reliability has been obtained.	
Construct validity	Constructs of academic reading, listening, and online composing can be reflected in computer-assisted test tasks. Open-ended responses are less likely than multiple-choice to be affected by systematic test-taking strategies.	The types of items that can be developed in computer-assisted formats are different from those that can be developed with other media. Performance on a computer-delivered test may fail to reflect the same ability as that which would be measured by other forms of assessment. Selection of items to be included on an adaptive test by an algorithm may not result in an appropriate sample of test content. Computer-assisted response scoring may fail to assign credit to the qualities of a response that are relevant to the construct that the test is intended to measure.
Authenticity	Computer-assisted test tasks simulate some tasks in the target language use domain.	Computer-assisted test tasks are dissimilar to some tasks in the target language use domain.
Interactiveness	Multimedia input may offer opportunities for enhanced interactiveness.	Short items sometimes used on computer-adaptive tests may limit interactiveness.

Table 5.4 *(continued)*

Quality	Positive attributes	Negative attributes
Impact	Anticipation of CALT should prompt computer work in L2 classes, which may help L2 learners gain important skills.	Tests may cause anxiety for examinees who do not have extensive experience using technology.
	Language programs may be prompted to make computers available to learners and teachers.	Tests may be so expensive that some examinees may not be able to take them.
		The research, development, and delivery infrastructure for CALT may funnel testing resources to technology in lieu of other, at least equally important, research areas.
Practicality	Computational analysis of responses makes open-ended questions a possibility for an operational testing program.	It may be too expensive to prepare the partial-credit scoring for items on a regular basis.
	Internet-delivered tests add flexibility of time and place for test delivery.	Internet-delivered tests can raise questions about test security in high-stakes testing.

correct, and therefore a rubric resulting in partial-credit scores implemented by computer should provide more precise measurement. Conceptually, this increase in reliability over dichotomously scored items reflects precision of measurement because the scores better reflect the examinees' knowledge, which we assume would frequently fall somewhere on a continuum from none to complete rather than at one end of the continuum. Empirically, the larger variance produced by partial-credit scores would produce a higher coefficient-alpha reliability. On tests with constructed responses, reliability in the rating process is typically a concern as well, but when scoring is done by a computer program, there is little question that the scoring will be done consistently from one rating to the next. This is a second positive point under the quality of reliability.

An additional positive quality concerning reliability is the potential of CATs to continue testing until a reliable score is obtained. The aim of the adaptivity in CAT is to provide the examinee with test items that are at an appropriate level of difficulty in order to obtain a reliable estimate of ability with as few items as possible. The CAT procedure challenges the common wisdom – the longer the test, the higher the reliability – by producing shorter tests with potentially equivalent or greater reliability. The new wisdom about test development and reliability cannot be expressed in terms of test length, but instead might be restated as, *the better the items fit the examinees, the higher the reliability*.

Construct validity

Construct validity was discussed in Chapter 3 from the perspective of threats posed by technology. These concerns are summarized on the negative side of construct validity in Table 5.4. The specific potential negative identified in the examples examined by Chapelle was that constraints placed on computer-adaptive testing can prescribe test tasks, making them poor measures of textual competence. The example was a computer-adaptive measure of ESL reading that did not contain reading passages (of a complete paragraph or more of connected text) but instead consisted of items with one to three sentences, which examinees were to read and respond to by selecting one of four responses (Madsen, 1991). More generally, the issue is that the types of items that can be developed in computer-assisted formats are different from those that can be developed with other media. In this case, the short items were intended to adhere to the assumption of independence required by the IRT model used to calculate the item parameters for the test, but another example from Chapter 3 would be reading tasks requiring the examinee to read from the screen rather than from paper, or to listen by clicking on a button on the screen rather than having the aural input controlled externally.

Other potential technology-related negatives are also associated with computer-adaptive testing. Selection of items to be included on an adaptive test by an algorithm may not result in an appropriate sample of test content. With respect to response analysis, computer-assisted response scoring may fail to assign credit to the qualities of a response that are relevant to the construct that the test is intended to measure. And finally, performance on a computer-delivered test may fail to reflect the same ability that would be measured by other forms of assessment. All of these issues, in addition to research intended to mitigate the problems, are discussed in Chapter 3, but the usefulness analysis prompts researchers to examine the other side of the construct validity analysis – the positive side.

The positive side of the construct-validity analysis is evident if we consider the fact that much of the language use that examinees engage in takes place through technology. In an environment where language users spend much of their time reading and writing in front of the computer, the constructs of academic reading, listening, and online composing might best be reflected in computer-assisted test tasks. So integral is the computer to the writing process that the idea of assessing writing ability with a paper-and-pencil writing task would be recognized by most academics as introducing bias into the measurement. Other abilities are less uniformly expressed through technology, and so the construct of interest has to be analyzed carefully, but most would agree that the use of open-ended responses in addition to multiple-choice responses is essential for construct validity in many language assessments, in part because open-ended responses are less likely than multiple-choice to be affected by systematic test-taking strategies (i.e., test wiseness). The use of computer algorithms to score such responses may make this response format useable, thereby increasing the potential for construct validity.

Authenticity

Some issues related to construct validity are also evident in the analysis of authenticity. Like the positive observation that the construct of composing online can best be measured through computer-assisted writing tasks, the positive side of authenticity analysis points to the fact that many computer-assisted test tasks simulate some academic tasks. The authenticity analysis requires the researcher to examine the types of tasks and uses of language that examinees will be engaged in beyond the test setting. The fact that much language use takes place through technology means that authentic language assessment tasks likewise need to engage examinees in language use through technology. But on the other hand, language use continues to occur without technology: language users still need to speak to people face to face, read paper books, and listen to live lectures; therefore, tasks reflecting these language uses have not become irrelevant to language assessment. What technology has done is to expand the options that language users have for selecting the mode of communication that they deem most effective, and because it is not always the test taker who will be able to exercise the choice, typically a range of modalities may be important to maintain in language tests if they are to be authentic in relation to a target language use context.

Interactiveness

Since interactiveness involves the engagement of the user's language and communication strategies, topical knowledge, and affective variables in an integrative way, the types of test tasks that can be constructed through dynamic multimedia presentations are potentially a positive feature within this category. In any particular test, of course, the extent to which such interactiveness is desirable depends on what the test is intended to measure. On the negative side, however, the short items sometimes used on computer-adaptive tests may limit interactiveness. To date, the limits of potential interactiveness in CALT have not been explored as they have in other areas such as video games, where the engagement of the user is also essential.

Impact

One of the threats of CALT discussed in Chapter 3 was the possibility that CALT may have a negative impact on learners, learning, classes, and society. Those negative consequences might come in the form of anxiety for examinees who do not have extensive experience using technology. This was the concern of Madsen (1986) over 20 years ago when the ESL CAT was introduced. Moreover, computer-based tests that incorporate many of the positive qualities of authenticity and reliability may be so expensive that some examinees cannot afford to take them. On the one hand, this is typically seen as an issue of practicality, from the perspective of the test developer, but for the individual who cannot apply to a university because the test is beyond his or her financial means, the negative consequences represent much more than that. At the level of the testing program, the research, development, and delivery infrastructure for CALT may funnel testing resources to technology in lieu of other, at least equally important, research areas. On the positive side of the impact issue, anticipation of CALT should prompt computer work in L2 classes, which may help L2 learners gain important skills in view of the reality of language use through technology today. Moreover, language programs may be prompted to make computers available to learners and teachers.

Practicality

The quality of practicality points to the need to consider the technical capabilities of test developers in view of what is required to develop and modify tests. Fulcher's detailed list of considerations helps to paint an accurate picture: that it requires the considerable expertise of staff to develop and implement CALT. Expertise costs money, and so does equipment and maintenance. A rule of thumb for technology projects is that they typically take longer and cost more than expected; therefore, the best advice is to start small and plan as carefully as possible. Our observation has been that CALT projects are often launched without the necessary expertise because such expertise is very difficult to find within the profession. However, even when expertise is available, decisions have to be made about whether or not authoring software is going to be developed, how sophisticated the input, response options, and interaction between input and response will be, and what procedures should be put into place to keep the work flow moving forward in a coordinated fashion. Beginning CALT developers would hope for some prescriptive advice about time, cost, and types of expertise needed, but in fact the variables are so numerous and interact in different ways across contexts, that any general advice risks failing to account for relevant factors. In our view, what is needed is the development of practice-based expertise in using and developing CALT by graduate students in applied linguistics so that their knowledge can be brought to bear on the ever-changing technology issues.

The value of a usefulness analysis for evaluating CALT is that the evaluation covers the same ground as does the evaluation of any test. It does not allow the technology to become a distraction, leaving aside the fundamentals of validation practices. The problem with doing so, however, is the risk of an evaluation scheme that glosses over and misses the very aspects of CALT that need to be considered because of the computer technology. To some extent such a usefulness analysis misses some of the important points that were highlighted by Noijons and Fulcher, and it may fail to challenge the field in the way that Meunier and Laurier attempted to do by highlighting unique technological potentials rather than the standard evaluation criteria. What is needed is a scheme that not only encompasses the concerns of educational measurement researchers more generally, but also integrates the concerns raised by the unique capabilities of the technology.

Validation and CALT

One would hope that the technology-specific concerns of CALT evaluation could be integrated into the larger context of validation theory. However, validation theory itself is somewhat of a moving target (Kane, 1992, 2001; Kane, Crooks & Cohen, 1999). Like the evolving technology scene, and perhaps prompted by technology to some extent, validation theory is undergoing change in ways that are likely to affect practice. At least two aspects of these changes may be important for conceptualizing CALT evaluation in the future: the argument-based structure for expressing aspects of evaluation, and the use-driven framework for demonstrating appropriate use.

An argument-based structure

Current work in educational measurement, which has influenced language testing, proposes that validation be framed within an argument-based structure for clarifying the basis for score meaning and use (Kane, 1992). For example, does a low score on the reading test of interest signify that the examinee indeed has a low level of reading ability? In argument-based terminology, that the examinee has a low level of reading ability is a *claim* that one might hope to make on the basis of the reading test score. The score itself does not prove with all certainty that the examinee's reading level is low. Instead, the test user infers on the basis of the test score that the reading ability is low, and the argument is developed when the testing researcher provides the necessary support for making such an interpretation. One approach to stating an argument, as explained by Bachman (in press), is the following:

> An observed score should be inferred to mean [claim], unless [there is some good reason].

This general form might be used to express the score meaning of a CALT reading test as follows:

> An observed low score on the CALT reading test should be inferred to mean an examinee has a low level of reading ability unless reading on a computer screen negatively affects performance so that examinees consistently score lower on CALT reading tasks than on paper-based reading tasks.

This formulation of the argument is constructed with the following:

[claim] = the examinee has a low level of reading ability
[the good reason] = reading on a computer screen negatively affects performance so examinees consistently score lower on CALT reading tasks than on paper-based reading tasks

The argument-based structure is well suited to the logic underlying investigations that focus on threats to validity as described in Chapter 3. For example, Figure 5.1 illustrates the argument structure that would be developed to interpret research addressing a threat. It consists of the test score in the box at the bottom and the inference denoted by the arrow pointing to the claim, "the examinee has a low level of reading ability." The "unless" arrow denotes a statement that would weaken the inference, which in this case is "reading on a computer screen negatively affects performance." The result from research is shown in the box below the "unless" statement as supporting that statement. In this example, these results refer to the research of Choi, Kim, and Boo (2003), discussed in Chapter 3. They found that the examinees scored lower on the computer-delivered version of their reading test, which was intended to provide equivalent scores to the paper test. This type of research is shown visually as supporting the *unless*-statement, demonstrating that *unless*-statements gain strength through such support.

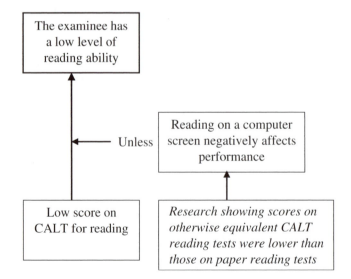

Figure 5.1 An example argument structure developed on the basis of a threat to validity.

Unless-statements in an argument can have more or less support depending on the nature of the research results and the number of studies that provide support. Stronger support for the *unless*-statement would be signified by multiple boxes with research results that support the *unless*-statement. Of course, strong support for the *unless*-statement indicates cause for not making the intended inference about the meaning of the test score. This is a more formal way of expressing the idea of a threat to the validity of test interpretation. Moreover, it includes a place for demonstrating the empirical support for the hypothesized threat. So, for example, one might place the idea that computer anxiety of the examinees negatively affects test scores in the position of an *unless*-statement, but without any evidence from research or observation to support the statement, it would not weaken the support for the intended inference.

On the left-hand side of the inference line, a *since*-statement can be placed in the argument as support for making the inference. A *since*-statement might be something like "the examinees have completed the tutorial on how to respond to test items," and support for that statement might be prior research showing that for examinees who have completed a tutorial teaching how to interact successfully with the computer interface reading performance is equivalent on computer and paper. In short, the argument structure provides the means of expressing the intended inference along with the statements ("since" and "unless") that would strengthen or weaken the inference, and the research supporting or failing to support the statements. The example shows that this structure can be used to place the types of threats that have been discussed and investigated into an argument pertaining to test score meaning, and therefore this approach connects the common-sense notion of a threat to the formal means of expressing score interpretation.

A use-driven framework

The interpretive argument, from Bachman's (in press) perspective, only completes the first part of the argument by clarifying score interpretation. In educational contexts, the crux of the issue is the decisions that are made on the basis of this interpretation, and consequently Bachman outlines what he calls a utilization argument, which is one part of an "assessment-use argument" that should support the use of a test for a particular purpose. Bachman (in press) describes the utilization argument through a framework that builds on the score interpretation (i.e., the result or conclusion from the interpretive argument).

The structure of the utilization argument is the same as it is for the interpretive argument, except that the beginning point is the score interpretation and the endpoint is the decision made on the basis of that interpretation. The score interpretation is shown in a dark box to denote that it is the same one that appeared in Figure 5.1. Figure 5.2 outlines the primary components of the utilization argument as conceived by Bachman (in press) using the example of the CALT reading test. In Figure 5.2 the utilization inference connects the interpretation of an examinee's low-level of reading ability to the decision of a placement in a low-level reading class. The interpretation was supported by the interpretive argument, and the utilization argument picks up where that left off to argue for a test use.

Bachman (in press) provides guidance about what types of considerations should appear in the *since*-statements of the utilization argument:

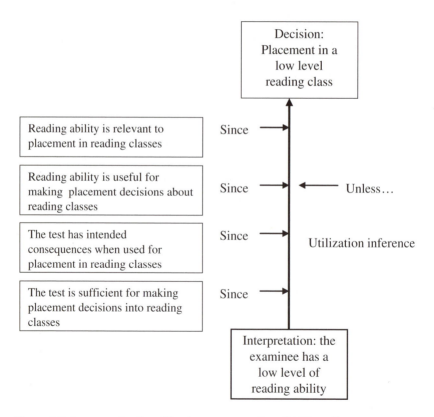

Figure 5.2 An example of a utilization argument for a CALT reading test.

relevance, utility, positive consequences, and sufficiency. Examples of such statements are shown in Figure 5.2, but the support that would back up each one is not illustrated in the interest of simplicity of the example. Such a utilization argument provides a means of including issues pertaining to real-world test use within an overall argument for test use. The particular *since*-statements offer a useful perspective on CALT. It is not unusual to hear an argument for CALT use that rests primarily on the statement of utility of decision making (e.g., placements based on the scores from a short, convenient, automatically scored test). Bachman's assessment-use argument illuminates the impotence of such an argument: An assessment-use argument needs to include an interpretive argument that clarifies the meaning (i.e., interpretation) of the test scores. This interpretation needs to serve as the starting point in a utilization argument consisting of evidence that backs up not only a statement about utility, but also statements about relevance, intended consequences, and sufficiency.

Time will tell how multifaceted technology concerns will intersect with aspects of these interpretive and utilization arguments. In the meantime, it seems clear that although technology adds some unique concerns in validation, ultimately these concerns need to be integrated within the overall argument for test score interpretation and use.

Conclusion

Both the usefulness analysis and the assessment-use argument offer ways of viewing CALT evaluation within a broader framework of validation. The usefulness argument highlights factors of particular concern in language assessment such as authenticity, which was raised by Meunier and by Laurier as a key issue for development and evaluation. The interpretive argument lays out the structure into which the specific test taking and interface concerns of Noijons and Fulcher can be situated, along with a variety of threats and concerns that might strengthen or weaken the basis for score interpretation. The utilization argument places the decision making aspect of testing at center stage to guide an analysis of evidence pertaining not only to utility but also to relevance, consequences, and sufficiency of test scores for a particular purpose.

At the same time, some CALT issues seem to escape notice within validation frameworks, particularly the integration of assessment into the learning process and use of tests in second language acquisition research. In these contexts, score interpretation remains important, but it is less clear that decision making should be the guiding force in a utilization argument. Instead, issues might include such factors as relevance, utility, sufficiency, and consequences for development and testing of theory for researchers or for promoting autonomous learning, for example. In the next chapter we will return to the issue of proactive thinking about technology in assessment as a direction worthy of further consideration.

CHAPTER SIX

The impact of CALT

Bennett, a measurement researcher and an enthusiastic advocate of technology, writes about the transformative impact of technology on large-scale educational assessment:

> New technology will permit [a] transformation [in assessment] by allowing us to create tests that are more firmly grounded in conceptualizations of what one needs to know and be able to do to succeed in a domain; by making performance assessment practical and routine through the use of computer-based simulation, automatic item generation, and automated essay scoring; and by changing the ways in which we deliver, and the purposes for which we use, large-scale tests. (Bennett, 1999a, p. 11)

The seeds for Bennett's enthusiasm about the transformative power of technology for assessment were planted much earlier, and many of these ideas have been hinted at by researchers in educational measurement for years (e.g., Bejar, 1985; Cole, 1993; Bejar & Braun, 1994). Although Bennett and other enthusiasts typically do not refer specifically to second language tests, they regularly include writing tests in their discussions. In reading these predictions, second language teachers, test developers, and researchers cannot help but consider whether or not our assessments are part of the revolution in assessment, and if so whether or not this revolution has happened, is in progress, or is yet to come.

In this chapter we will suggest that in second language assessment, despite the significant changes and advances made through the use of technology, the revolution portrayed by Bennett has not yet occurred.

Although automated scoring and computer-assisted test delivery are realities, we were unable to show evidence for performance assessment made practical through widespread use of simulation, authentic item generation, or significant changes in testing purposes through technology. Such revolutionary changes need to be prompted and supported by conceptual advances in our understanding of language, language use, and language learning. More than 15 years ago, Alderson made this point in his discussion of individualized classroom testing:

> Possibilities for diagnosis and remediation raise an important problem for applied linguists and language teachers. The limitation on the development of such tests is not the capacity of the hardware, or the complexity of the programming task, but our inadequate understanding of the nature of language learning and of language use . . . the challenge of [CALT] is more to the linguist and applied linguist to provide appropriate input on the nature of branching routines, and on the hints, clues and feedback that would help learners, than to the computer programmer to produce adequate software.
>
> (Alderson, 1990, p. 25)

Alderson was focusing on CALT in the service of classroom learning, but analogous comments could have been made about other types of tests as well. Today there is little evidence to suggest that great progress has been made toward building the specific types of knowledge that could fuel the revolution. In fact, the recent discussion of the DIALANG project (Alderson, 2005), a large-scale diagnostic computer-delivered test, makes the same point. DIALANG was developed on the basis of the levels of the Common European Framework, but because research on second language acquisition has not examined development of grammar and vocabulary in view of these levels, the would-be diagnosis of specific linguistic forms and functions does not have a clear basis in either theory or research. In this case, the attempt is being made to expand test uses radically by providing learners with diagnostic information that can give precise guidance about what to study; however, the professional knowledge of second language acquisition falls short of providing the basis for such a revolutionary change.

Despite the fact that the revolution has not occurred, in language-testing practice today the idea that technology has changed language testing holds some credibility. After all, many language tests are delivered by computer and books on every aspect of language assessment predict a profound role for technology in the future. On the surface, anyway, it seems that many test takers are affected by CALT. We would suggest that these changes would most appropriately be considered evolutionary, because they have not significantly advanced and changed the way testing is conducted or the ways tests are used. Instead, through the use of CALT, researchers have made incremental advances in addressing some of the perennial problems in language assessment. Rather than describing a revolution characterized by new types of tests and roles for testing, we have written about the evolutionary advances and the issues they have raised about test development and validation. In this chapter, we consider some of the implications of these advances for applied linguistics. We also suggest future directions and discuss what revolutionary changes might entail.

Advances in language assessment through CALT

In the previous chapters we have described CALT used in practice today, research intended to increase understanding of and improve CALT, methods used to develop CALT, and validation issues for CALT. The first chapter argued that technology plays such a significant role in everyday assessment practices that knowledge and an understanding of technology-related issues is essential for language teachers, professional test developers, and language-testing researchers.

Chapter 2 demonstrated the ways that CALT is being used in many testing programs and situations, expanding the test developer's options for constructing test tasks. We described ways in which technology affects the test method characteristics including physical and temporal test circumstances, the test rubric, input and response characteristics, the interaction between input and response, and the characteristics of assessment. We showed that the most salient differences are to be found in the characteristics of the input and response, the interaction between them, and assessment. Advances in test delivery and access were evident in the examples of rich contextualized input, the variety of response techniques, computer adaptivity, and automated scoring made possible by computer. However, we were unable to report on revolutionary changes such as performance assessment made practical through the use of simulations.

In Chapter 3, we discussed the potential problems raised by CALT in terms of the way they affect validity. We noted six concerns that are often expressed as potential threats of CALT: different test performance, new task types, limitations due to adaptive item selection, inaccurate automatic scoring, compromised security, and negative impact. We noted that few studies have attempted to better understand the meaning of test scores from CALT and the consequences of CALT use. We also noted that the potential threats to validity were framed in terms of suspicions about how technology might undermine the validity or fairness of testing. In other words, the most public discussion of CALT has been framed by a skeptical view that asks how technology might undermine current practices rather than an innovative perspective that seeks to discover how technology can contribute to a revolution which significantly improves the overall usefulness of assessment.

In Chapter 4, we discussed how would-be CALT developers might work with authoring tools such as WebCT, pointing out that the tools required for test development depend on the purpose of the assessment and such practical issues as the resources of time, money and expertise. The reality of language assessment is that limitations in money and expertise for developing authoring tools specific to language assessment limit the degree to which revolutionary innovations are likely to be developed. Consequently, ideal authoring systems have not been developed for language assessments, but this is an active area of inquiry.

Chapter 5 suggested that computer-based testing should be evaluated against standards that are consistent with those used to evaluate other tests, but that technology-related issues need to be highlighted. The specific technology-related issues identified by CALT researchers should be placed within a broader framework of test evaluation, focusing on aspects of test usefulness, which highlights factors of particular concern in language assessment such as authenticity as a key issue for test development and evaluation. We explored an interpretive argument which laid out a structure into which specific test-taking and interface concerns might be situated. However, this discussion was necessarily tentative in view of the limited amount of research reported on empirical validation of CALT from current perspectives.

In sum, the reality of CALT today is not what one could call a revolution in language assessment. Certain characteristics of CALT methods are substantively different from those of tests involving other means of delivery and response, but technology has not radically reconfigured the role of assessment in teaching and learning. Thus far we have seen CALT as an evolution in assessment, expanding what we do in testing, rather than a revolution, changing what assessment is in relation to language education and research. A revolution may be coming sometime in the future, but in the meantime, in view of the central role that language assessment plays in applied linguistics, the changes brought about by technology intersect in important ways with other areas of applied linguistics.

CALT in applied linguistics

The development, use, and evaluation of CALT challenges and expands the imaginations of applied linguists because of the new options opened by testing through technology. One issue is the need to consider the nature of the language abilities that are called upon in technology-mediated interactions and communication, and therefore, the need to rethink test constructs. A second issue is that the precision of the information about learners that can be analyzed on the basis of examinees' constructed test responses prompts test designers to consider what to do with such capabilities. For example, should test developers reconsider how research on SLA can inform the development of tests that provide more detailed information than tests relying on human raters? A third issue is that the flexibility of the technology for anytime, anywhere testing and record keeping appears to afford powerful opportunities for improving instruction through assessment. These three issues, which have persisted throughout this volume, are worthy of additional discussion.

Language ability and use

Investigation of CALT underscores the fact that the language constructs underlying score interpretation need to be considered in view of the context in which the language is used. Applied linguists would therefore speak of language ability as the ability to choose and deploy appropriate linguistic resources for particular types of situations. But today we might replace such a conception of language ability with one that encompasses the ability to select and deploy appropriate language through the technologies that are appropriate for a situation. Email is good for some things; a phone call or a face-to-face conversation is better for others. The language user often makes the choice. The spell-checker is informative sometimes; it needs to be ignored at others. The language user makes the choice. These choices ultimately depend on the language user's technological and strategic competence, which together with linguistic competence may be the type of construct of relevance to language use through technology.

In other words, communicative language ability needs to be conceived in view of the joint role that language and technology play in the process of communication. Rassool (1999) brings communicative competence into the modern era by suggesting that "communicative competence refers to the interactive process in which meanings are produced dynamically between information technology and the world in which we live" (p. 238). From the perspective of language assessment this statement raises the polemical issue of a context-dependent language construct. Literacy researchers such as Tyner (1998) begin to explore what this could mean: they see the need to splinter the construct of literacy to express their belief that technology affects the nature of literacy required for language use *with different technologies*:

> New approaches to literacy teaching and learning suggest that instead of approaching literacy as a monolithic concept . . . it is more useful to break literacy down into any number of multiple literacy modes, each with distinctive characteristics that reveal a variety of social purposes . . . These multiple literacies have been called *technology literacy, information literacy, visual literacy, media literacy,* and so on . . . As contemporary communication media converge into sensory soup, the particular features of each of these literacies also converge and overlap . . .   (Tyner, 1998, p. 60)

Such a proliferation of literacies may reduce the term to denote any ability, whether or not it entails language. The implication for language assessment is not completely clear. However, the idea that various technologies might affect the abilities of interest in language assessment seems like an issue that needs to be considered in the process of test development and validation today whether or not CALT is involved. Bruce and Hogan (1998) express this idea in terms of technology being an integral part of communication: they point out that anyone who is not competent in using the technology is not competent in communication in many important situations. A similar issue is evident in attempts to define a construct underlying a test of language for specific purposes. It is both the specific purpose knowledge and the linguistic and strategic competence that work together to accomplish communication (Douglas, 2000). Likewise, it is probably the combination of language and strategic competence together with technological knowledge that accomplishes communication through technology.

Elaborating on the view of multiple technology-defined literacies, Warschauer argues that the literacy skills learners need to acquire in today's world are qualitatively different from those they need to participate in literate life that does not involve technology. Warschauer (2000) describes new language and literacy skills needed for effective communication by replacing the constructs of reading and writing with the abilities that he refers to as reading/research and writing/authorship, respectively (p. 521). These constructs, which include aspects of the strategic competence required to perform successfully in some electronic environments, force test developers and users to confront how strategic competence is to come into play. This is not a new problem, but it is one that is exposed and amplified through CALT. In this way, CALT provides both the need and the opportunity to better understand the language abilities called upon in computer-mediated communication. In terms of the interpretive argument explained in Chapter 5, the test developer would need to express the score interpretation in terms of ability to gather visually presented information on the Internet rather than in terms such as "reading ability" in general.

In attempting to formulate theory-based perspectives on the abilities required for use of language through technology, language-testing researchers face the challenge of integrating the seemingly incompatible discourses of language assessment and literacy studies. Literacy studies take a social practice perspective entailing description of behavior rather than the more cognitive perspective that underlies much language assessment work. From the perspective of social practice, electronic literacy and multimodal literacy, for example, are seen as what people do with language through technology rather than what they need to know about language and the strategies they need to use language through technology. Some argue that an ability perspective is incommensurable with the social practice perspective of new literacy studies because the former typically entails defining a theoretical ability that is responsible for performance across contexts, and the latter is based on description of specific context-based performances. It may be that exploration of interpretive arguments for CALT will prompt applied linguists to better understand the abilities underlying electronic literacy, or multimodal literacy, in a manner that is measurable and that yields interpretable and useful scores.

Second language acquisition

Development and evaluation of CALT underscores the need to strengthen connections between second language acquisition (SLA) and language assessment. Anyone who has attempted to design the specifics of testing method for a computer-delivered test or to tackle the problem of assigning partial-score values to examinee responses can grasp the issue at stake. In providing written or aural input to the examinee, should help be offered as well? In assigning a score from one to six to a written essay, what makes a five better than a four? What are the specific linguistic, rhetorical, and content features that prompt the assignment of a particular score on the six-point scale? In developing a rationale for issues such as these, one would hope that theory and research on SLA would be informative in at least three ways.

First, it would seem that research investigating developmental sequences of acquisition should play a role in developing and scoring some assessments in which grammar plays a role in performance. For example, Norris (in press) wrote items for a grammar-screening test on the basis of studies in SLA that have demonstrated the relatively earlier development of some grammatical knowledge over other aspects. Low-level examinees were expected to perform better on items requiring the ordering of words in single-clause declarative sentences than on items requiring ordering of words in sentences with embedded noun clauses. These items were scored as either correct or incorrect, and no linguistic production was scored, but one would hope to be able to explore the analysis of learner's production in light of work in SLA.

In Chapter 3 we discussed the tension felt by test developers in need of rationales underlying procedures for scoring responses with multiple possible responses. Even the non-linguistic responses of the text-sequencing task investigated by Alderson, Percsich, and Szabo (2000) needed to have a basis for assigning the scores to the many various orderings that the examinees might give. But the issue was exacerbated by the enormous variations that might be entered by examinees taking Coniam's (1998) dictation test, which used an automatic scoring routine, the reading test with open-ended responses developed by Jamieson, Campbell, Norfleet, and Berbisada (1993), or the essays discussed by Powers, Burstein, Chodorow, Fowles, and Kukich (2001). In all of these cases, and many more that we might imagine, the developers should benefit from a scientific basis upon which they can consider some performance as evidence of advanced knowledge and some other performance as lower level. Ideally, some professional knowledge about acquisition could be drawn upon for CALT.

The work that has attempted to identify linguistic features associated with levels of ESL writing might offer some suggestions for developing rationales for response analysis in assessment. Wolfe-Quintero, Inagaki, and Kim (1998) review the issues and findings of research seeking syntactic performance indicative of levels on a developmental index; they consider development along the dimensions of fluency, accuracy, and complexity. Hinkel (2003) identifies lexical choices made by ESL writers that contribute to the perception of simplistic and imprecise writing. Both of these lines of research appear to be productive in developing a better understanding of levels of performance. At the same time, such research is necessarily limited if it is interpreted as suggesting that linguistic knowledge is acquired in an invariant order or that linguistic knowledge is impervious to the conditions under which it is displayed. Without disregarding empirical results that provide evidence for more, or less, linguistic knowledge, language-testing researchers need to take into account the cognitive and contextual factors that also come into play during performance.

A second way in which SLA research might fruitfully inform test development and response scoring is through research identifying the effects of processing conditions on performance. The assumption underlying this strand of SLA research is that performance needs to be explained in view of not only the knowledge of the examinee, but also the conditions under which performance was obtained. Researchers such as Skehan (1998) and Robinson (2001) therefore hypothesize particular task characteristics that should be expected to produce more, or less, difficult conditions for performance. For example, a requirement to produce a written response quickly vs. slowly would interact with the examinee's level of linguistic knowledge to produce a higher or lower level of response. In other words, dimensions other than level of knowledge need to be taken into account in interpreting performance.

A third dimension that needs to be integrated is the context constructed for the examinee's performance. The extended language production desired in tests involving speaking and writing is produced in response to a prompt intending to create a particular contextual configuration (Halliday & Hasan, 1989) for the examinee. This in turn cues the examinee to produce genre-appropriate language to accomplish a communicative function (Paltridge, 2001). Such tests, if they are well designed, help the examinee to understand and create a discourse domain (Douglas, 2000), which includes the topic of the response, the audience, and its communicative function. As a consequence, the job of analyzing the language produced on such tasks is not at all an open-ended, general problem of language analysis, but rather a problem that can be characterized empirically by the functional grammarian's description (e.g., Halliday, 1994) of the ways in which learners at various levels of ability deploy their limited linguistic resources to construct meaning in a well-defined context. This is the type of work that has been conducted in computational linguistics and artificial intelligence for over 40 years, except that such research has been concerned with typical proficient-speakers' performance in defined contexts rather than levels of learners' performance.

Working toward a better understanding of these three factors in shaping test performance seems to be an essential step for today's machine-scored assessments as well as for the more revolutionary intelligent assessment of the future. Bennett (1999b) describes "intelligent assessment" (p. 99) as an integration of three lines of research: constructed-response testing, artificial intelligence, and model-based measurement. He explained:

> This integration is envisioned as producing assessment methods consisting of tasks closer to the complex problems typically encountered in academic and work settings. These tasks will be scored by automated routines that emulate the behavior of an expert, providing a rating on a partial credit scale for summative purposes as well as a qualitative description designed to impart instructionally useful information. The driving mechanisms underlying these tasks and their scoring are . . . measurement models [grounded in cognitive psychology] that may dictate what the characteristics of the items should be, which items from a large pool should be administered, how item responses should be combined to make more general inferences, and how uncertainty should be handled.   (p. 99)

To support such research in second language testing, however, would require substantial collaboration between language assessment and SLA at least in the three areas outlined above. Such connections are not altogether implausible (e.g., Brown, Hudson, Norris & Bonk, 2002) despite the fact that the two areas of applied linguistics seem to speak different languages. Even the most basic working constructs such as units of analysis are different, with assessment researchers talking about reading, writing, listening, speaking, and SLA researchers talking about the tense and aspect system, the negation system, or polite requests, for example. Attempts to bring measurement concepts to bear on the complex data of interest in SLA (e.g., Chapelle, 1996; Bachman & Cohen, 1998) need to be developed into a more systematic program of research. This is what Norris and Ortega (2003) suggest in their review of measurement practices in SLA: The SLA community needs to "engage in a comprehensive approach to all of the stages in the measurement process [in order to] find itself much better able to make theoretically meaningful interpretations about constructs and to pursue the accumulation of scientifically worthwhile knowledge" (p. 749).

For such knowledge to ultimately inform the design of CALT, however, language-testing researchers need to be able to distinguish between the SLA knowledge connected to theoretical debates in SLA and that which can inform assessment. An analogous distinction has usefully been made in SLA in general and the more focused area of "instructed SLA." The latter focuses on the conditions for language performance and acquisition that pertain to instructional decisions. Of particular relevance is research aimed at increasing the research-based knowledge about pedagogic tasks (e.g., Crookes & Gass, 1993; Bygate, Skehan & Swain, 2003). It is this area that is appropriately focused to serve as a basis for hypotheses and empirical research about computer assisted language learning (CALL). Similarly, an area that one might call "assessed SLA" is needed to focus on aspects of acquisition that can be empirically observed in performance under particular cognitive conditions and in defined contexts.

Language teaching

In the first chapter we suggested that language teachers need a solid understanding of assessment because they help learners to develop self-assessment strategies, test learners in the classroom, select or develop tests for language programs, and prepare learners to take tests beyond the classroom and language program. However, perhaps the most provocative vision for language assessment in the classroom is the potential for assessments to help students to become better, more autonomous learners.

In Chapter 2, we described some examples of CALL programs such as Longman English Interactive, and Market Leader that contained testing and feedback to learners within the instructional packages. The idea is that if learners can be regularly informed about the quality of their knowledge and progress as they proceed through instruction, they can make better choices about studying, and ultimately become more self-reliant. Of course, if these capabilities are to be implemented, courseware developers need to have a firm understanding of the principles of assessment in the service of learning.

Moreover, assessments are not necessarily used simply because publishers have produced them. Teachers need to learn about the potentials of computer-assisted assessment if they are to introduce them to learners.

In other words, the divide that seems to exist between language testers and language teachers is dysfunctional with respect to the aim of expanding the uses of assessment in revolutionary ways. Stoynoff and Chapelle (2005) argue that it is essential to move beyond this divide and that language teachers need to become assessment literate in order to select and construct tests for learners. The potential of new uses for assessments integrated into computer-assisted learning materials creates an additional motivation for teachers' assessment literacy. In this respect, CALT might be seen as providing a powerful opportunity for positive impact within the profession that goes beyond the types of washback that have been the focus of recent research (e.g., Cheng, Watanabe & Curtis, 2004).

Future directions

Today's CALT raises issues that must be explored if it is to evolve sufficiently to become part of a revolution in assessment. Current technologies represent an embarrassment of riches for test developers – from test delivery at a distance, precise control over timing and multimedia input for examinees to natural language processing and student models. The tools for test building have become extremely sophisticated. If test developers are to make appropriate use of such tools, research needs to be guided by a clear agenda in applied linguistics which is supported by cross-disciplinary knowledge.

A cross-disciplinary project

Although the precise issues raised by technology fall squarely within the domain of problems that applied linguists should know how to address, the tools for addressing them need to be developed and tested in an arena where cross-disciplinary collaboration is brought to bear on the issues. In Chapter 4 we discussed authoring tools such as WebCT, Respondus, Hot Potatoes, Quiz Center, Blackboard, and Questionmark. Whereas these systems provide tools for developing tests in general, we saw that they did not contain specific language-related features, most notably capture of spoken linguistic responses and a means of analyzing constructed responses to assign a rationale-based partial score. Software tools specific to the needs of second language testing need to be developed based on the limitations of existing tools for language testing.

Teachers and software developers have been creating individual tests using general purpose authoring or specific programming languages for over 30 years (e.g., Boyle, Smith & Eckert, 1976). However, if this experience and knowledge base is to be developed in a cumulative fashion, professional quality authoring tools are needed for the applied linguistic community to use. Development of a robust set of appropriate tools requires a group of professionals comprising at least software engineers, language assessment specialists, and designers. Without the basic software tools that graduate students can use to learn about testing, it seems that the level of discussion about test design is confined to a level of unprofessional speculation about what *might* work and what *would be* interesting. For example, the Dutch CEF Construct Project (Alderson, Figueres, Kuijper, Nold, Takala & Tardieu, 2004) is an example of a piece of software that is intended to help test designers develop and analyze test tasks according to a construct-based framework (like the Common European Framework of Reference – CEFR). Projects such as DIALANG have taken some steps to develop a variety of item types and hopefully will develop authoring tools as well that will allow other authors to experiment with them (Alderson, 2005).

Other glimpses of what is possible with sophisticated software can be found in papers about intelligent computer-assisted language learning (e.g., Chanier, Pengelly, Twidale & Self, 1992), which are the product of such cross-disciplinary research. Such a system contains the elements similar to those Bennett described as essential for intelligent assessment – analysis of learners' constructed responses, a student model which is updated on the basis of analysis of examinees' responses, and an expert system that selects probes for the learner to gain more information. It is not clear to what extent any measurement concepts come into play in this system, which is not intended specifically for assessment. But the point is that such complex systems are being explored in other areas, and that making them accessible to researchers in language assessment requires more sophisticated authoring tools than those which one finds for developing classroom tests.

An applied linguistics agenda

Despite the need to draw on expertise across the areas of educational measurement, applied linguistics, second language acquisition, and technology, the agenda needs to be set and driven by the concerns of applied linguists for assessment. However, even within applied linguistics, a carefully articulated stance needs to be developed toward technology. Based on analysis of approaches toward developing agendas for research and practice in language assessment, Chapelle (2003) identifies three approaches that are taken, as summarized in Table 6.1.

The tunnel approach, as in "tunnel vision," refers to a metaphor from Brown and Duguid (2000), who describe technologists across all facets of society as moving single-mindedly to goals of speed and efficiency without regard for anything else. In language assessment, technology is often construed in this way – as a means of constructing more efficient tests. If efficiency is the goal, the desired results are shorter, more convenient tests. In other words, the argument to be made by test developers is that the computer-based test can do the same thing as the tests offered in other forms, except faster and cheaper.

A comparison approach to CALT treats the technology as suspect, and therefore the problem for research is to discern the differences between computer-based tests and other types of tests. Such analyses can be conducted at the level of performance on a whole test or it can be studied at the level of item performance. What underlies this perspective, however, is the view that the no-technology condition is the normal one, and then the problem is to figure out what difference the technology makes. Both the tunnel and the comparison approaches clearly seek to achieve worthwhile goals. In applied linguistics, who would suggest that more efficient

Table 6.1 *Assumptions about technology and results of tunnel, comparison, and innovation approaches (From Chapelle, 2003, p. 179)*

Approach	Assumption about technology in assessment	Results
Tunnel	It is an efficiency	Short tests with automatic scoring and delivery of results for existing test uses
Comparison	It should be considered suspect	A variety of types of tests for existing test uses; knowledge about how technology affects traditional tests when they are delivered online
Innovation	It should be considered a resource	A variety of types of tests and new test uses; knowledge about the intersection of technology with a variety of assessment issues

and convenient tests are not desired? Who would deny the value of better understanding how technology affects performance conditions and test results? However, while these two perspectives are clearly in line with applied linguistics and language assessment, each is limited in its capacity to revolutionize language assessment in the ways that Bennett described.

The revolution may lie within the innovative approach, which draws on technology as a resource to explore a variety of assessment issues. Chapelle (2003) suggests that such innovation entails development of a variety of tests and test uses that are not possible without technology. To do so would require the types of language testing software tools mentioned above, and should also entail the use of technology for developing knowledge about the intersection of technology with a variety of assessment issues. Educational measurement researcher Eva Baker suggests that such an agenda of innovation is at the heart of the revolution in which technology is to play an important role. She argues that "Technology applied to the service of understanding the learning we want will help us fix the presently unfixable – the deep validity problem at the heart of our testing system" (Baker, 1998, p. 22).

Conclusion

The suggestions and questions that appear within an innovative approach to CALT are many of the same ones posed by the pioneer-innovators in this area over ten years ago. Canale (1986) suggested the use of intelligent tutoring technologies to model learners' knowledge and inform instruction. Alderson (1988) pointed out that the computer can make use of language rules for analysis of learners' constructed responses. Corbel (1993) asked about the possibilities of intelligent assessment, CALT to aid in self-assessment, and strengthening links between assessment and other areas of applied linguistics through technology. Despite the evolutionary developments in assessment that have incorporated technology, we are not able to report on any revolutionary changes in assessment that might have resulted from systematic inquiry into these areas. Computer technology may in the future radically change research and practice in language assessment but doing so will require the type of research that engages with the complexity of the issues, crossing the boundaries between assessment, language, and technology for the purpose of developing paths that work toward the goals of applied linguists.

References

Ackerman, T. (1994). Creating a test information profile for a two-dimensional latent space. *Applied Psychological Measurement, 18*(3), 257–75.

ACT Inc. (2004). Web Page: http://www.act.org/esl/sample/grammar4.html. Accessed 11 January 2005.

Alderson, J. C. (1980). Scoring procedures for use on cloze tests. In C. A. Yorio, K. Perkins & J. Schacter (eds.), *On TESOL '79* (pp. 193–205). Washington, DC: TESOL Publications.

Alderson, J. C. (1988). *Innovations in language testing: Can the microcomputer help?* Special Report No 1 *Language Testing Update.* Lancaster, UK: University of Lancaster.

Alderson, J. C. (1990). Learner-centered testing through computers: Institutional issues in individual assessment. In J. de Jong & D. K. Stevenson (eds.) *Individualizing the assessment of language abilities* (pp. 20–7). Clevedon, UK: Multilingual Matters.

Alderson, J. C. (2000). *Assessing reading.* Cambridge: Cambridge University Press.

Alderson, J. C. (2005). *Diagnosing foreign language proficiency: The interface between learning and assessment.* London: Continuum.

Alderson, J.C., Figueras, N., Kuijper, H., Nold, G., Takala, S. & Tardieu, C. (2004). *The development of specifications for item development and classification within the Common European Framework of Reference for Languages: Learning, Teaching, Assessment, Reading and Listening.* Final Report of The Dutch CEF Construct Project. Mimeo.

Alderson, J. C. & Hamp-Lyons, L. (1996). TOEFL preparation courses: a study of washback. *Language Testing, 13*(3), 280–297.

Alderson, J. C., Percsich, R. & Szabo, G. (2000). Sequencing as an item type. *Language Testing, 17*(4), 423–47.

Alderson, J. C. & Wall, D. (1993). Does washback exist? *Applied Linguistics, 14,* 115–29.

Alessi, S. M. & Trollop, S. R. (1985). *Computer-based instruction: Methods and development.* Englewood Cliffs, NJ: Prentice-Hall.

Almond, R. G., Steinberg, L. S. & Mislevy, R. J. (2002). Enhancing the design and delivery of assessment systems: A four-process architecture. *Journal of Technology, Learning and Assessment, 1*(5), Available from http://www.jtla.org.

American Educational Research Association, American Psychological Association, National Council on Measurement in Education (1999). *Standards for educational and psychological testing.* Washington, DC: American Psychological Association.

Bachman, L.F. (1990). *Fundamental considerations in language testing.* Oxford: Oxford University Press.

Bachman, L. F. (1991). What does language testing have to offer? *TESOL Quarterly, 25*(4), 671–704.

Bachman, L. F. & Palmer, A. S. (1996). *Language testing in practice.* Oxford: Oxford University Press.

Bachman, L. F. (2000). Modern language testing at the turn of the century: assuring that what we count counts. *Language Testing, 17*(1), 1–42.

Bachman, L. F. (2004). *Statistical analyses for language assessment.* Cambridge: Cambridge University Press.

Bachman, L. F. (in press). Building and supporting a case for test use. *Language Assessment Quarterly.*

Bachman, L. F. & Cohen, A. D. (eds.) (1998). *Interfaces between second language acquisition and language testing research.* Cambridge: Cambridge University Press.

Bachman, L. F., Lynch, B. & Mason, M. (1995). Investigating variability in tasks and rater judgments in a performance test of foreign language speaking. *Language Testing, 12*(2), 238–58.

Bailey, K. (1996). Working for washback: A review of the washback concept in language testing. *Language Testing, 13*(3), 257–79.

Baker, E. L. (1998). *Understanding educational quality: Where validity meets technology. The fifth annual William Angoff Memorial Lecture.* Princeton, NJ: Educational Testing Service.

Baker, F. B. (1989). Computer technology in test construction and processing. In R. L. Linn (Ed.) *Educational measurement,* 3rd edn (pp. 409–28). NY: Macmillan Publishing Co.

Bejar, I. I. (1985). Speculations on the future of test design. In S. Embretson (ed.), *Test design — Developments in psychology and psychometrics* (pp. 279–94). Orlando: Academic Press.

Bejar, I. & Braun, H. (1994). On the synergy between assessment and instruction: Early lessons from computer-based simulations. *Machine-Mediated Learning, 4*(1), 5–25.

Bennett, R. E. (1993). On the meanings of constructed responses. In R. E. Bennett & W. C. Ward (eds.), *Construction versus choice in cognitive measurement: Issues in constructed response, performance testing, and portfolio assessment* (pp. 1–27). Hillsdale, NJ: Lawrence Erlbaum Associates.

Bennett, R. E. (1999a). How the Internet will help large-scale assessment reinvent itself. *Education Policy Analysis Archives, 9*(5), 1–25.

Bennett, R. E. (1999b). Using new technology to improve assessment. *Educational Measurement: Issues and Practice, 18*(3), 5–12.

Bennett, R. E. (2001). How the Internet will help large-scale assessment reinvent itself. *Educational Policy Analysis Archives, 9(5),* 1–27. Online: http://epaa. asu.edu/epaa/v9n5.html (Accessed 11 January 2005).

Birenbaum, M. & Tatsuoka, K. K. (1987). Open-ended versus multiple-choice response formats — It does make a difference for diagnostic purposes. *Applied Psychological Measurement, 11*(4), 385–95.

Blackboard. (2004). Blackboard Learning System. Blackboard, inc. http://www. blackboard.com (Accessed 11 January 2005).

Blais, J-G. & Laurier, M. D. (1993). The dimensionality of a placement test from several analytical perspectives. *Language Testing, 10*(2), 72–98.

Boyle, T. A., Smith, W. F. & Eckert, R. G. (1976). Computer-mediated testing: A branched program achievement test. *Modern Language Journal, 60,* 428–40.

Bradlow, E. T., Wainer, H. & Wang, X. (1999). A Bayesian random effects model for testlets. *Psychometrika, 64,* 153–68.

Brown, A. & Iwashita, N. (1996). The role of language background in the validation of a computer-adaptive test. *System, 24*(2), 199–206.

Brown, J. D. (1997). Computers in language testing: Present research and some future directions. *Language Learning & Technology, 1*(1), 44–59.

Brown, J. D., Hudson, T., Norris, J. & Bonk, W. J. (2002). *An investigation of second language task-based performance assessments, Technical Report #24.* Honolulu: Second Language Teaching & Curriculum Center, University of Hawaii at Manoa.

Brown, J. S. & Duguid, P. (2000). *The social life of information.* Boston, MA: Harvard Business School Press.

Bruce, B. C. & Hogan, M. P. (1998). The disappearance of technology: Toward an ecological model of literacy. In *Handbook of literacy and technology: Transformations in a post-typographic world* (pp. 269–81). Mahwah, NJ: Lawrence Erlbaum Associates.

Buck, G. (2001). *Assessing listening.* Cambridge: Cambridge University Press.

Burstein, J., Frase, L., Ginther, A. & Grant, L. (1996). Technologies for language assessment. *Annual Review of Applied Linguistics, 16,* 240–60.

Burston, J. & Monville-Burston, M. (1995). Practical design and implementation considerations of a computer-adaptive foreign language test: The Monash/ Melbourne French CAT. *CALICO Journal, 13*(1), 26–46.

Bygate, M., Skehan, P. & Swain, M. (eds.) (2003). *Researching pedagogic tasks: Second language learning, teaching, and testing.* Harrow, England: Longman.

Canale, M. (1986). The promise and threat of computerized adaptive assessment of reading comprehension. In C. Stansfield (ed.), *Technology and language testing* (pp. 30–45). Washington, DC: TESOL Publications.

Canale, M. (1987). Language assessment: the method is the message. In D. Tannen & J. E. Alatis (eds.), *The interdependence of theory, data, and application* (pp. 249–62). Washington, DC: Georgetown University Press.

Carr, N., Pan, M. & Xi, X. (2002). Construct refinement and automated scoring in web-based testing. Paper presented at the Language Testing Research Colloquium, Hong Kong, December 2002.

Carroll, J. B. (1968). The psychology of language testing. In A. Davies (ed.), *Language testing symposium: A Psycholinguistic Perspective* (pp. 46–69). Oxford: Oxford University Press.

Chalhoub-Deville, M. (ed.) (1999). *Development and research in computer adaptive language testing.* Cambridge: University of Cambridge Examinations Syndicate/Cambridge University Press.

Chalhoub-Deville, M. & Deville, C. (1999). Computer adaptive testing in second language contexts. *Annual Review of Applied Linguistics, 19,* 273–99.

Chanier, T., Pengelly, M., Twidale, M. & Self, J. (1992). Conceptual modelling in error analysis in computer-assisted language learning systems. In M. L. Swartz & M. Yazdani (eds.), *Intelligent tutoring systems for foreign language learning* (pp. 125–50). Berlin: Springer-Verlag.

Chapelle, C. A. (1993). Issues in computer-assisted analysis for one-word test responses. *Assessment — Transactions of the 1993 CALICO Symposium* (pp. 28–32). Durham, NC: CALICO.

Chapelle, C. A. (1996). Validity issues in computer-assisted strategy assessment. *Applied Language Learning, 7*(1), 47–60.

Chapelle, C. A. (1999). Validity in language assessment. *Annual Review of Applied Linguistics, 19,* 254–72.

Chapelle, C. A. (2001). *Computer applications in second language acquisition: Foundations for teaching, testing, and research.* Cambridge: Cambridge University Press.

Chapelle, C. A. (2003). *English language learning and technology: Lectures on applied linguistics in the age of information and communication technology.* Amsterdam: John Benjamins Publishing.

Chapelle, C. A. & Abraham, R. (1990). Cloze method: What difference does it make? *Language Testing, 7*(2), 121–45.

Chapelle, C. A., Enright, M. K. & Jamieson, J. (forthcoming). Challenges in developing a test of academic English. In C. A. Chapelle, M. K. Enright & J. Jamieson (eds.), *Building a validity argument for TOEFL.* Mahwah, NJ: Lawrence Erlbaum Associates.

Chapelle, C. A. & Jamieson, J. (2001). *Longman English Assessment.* White Plaines, NY: Pearson Education.

Chapelle, C. A., Jamieson, J. & Hegelheimer, V. (2003). Validation of a web-based ESL test. *Language Testing, 20*(4), 409–39.

Cheng, L., Watanabe, Y. & Curtis, A. (eds.) (2004). Washback in language testing: Research contexts and methods. Mahwah, NJ: Lawrence Erlbaum Associates.

Choi, I.-C., Kim, K. S. & Boo, J. (2003). Comparability of a paper-based language test and a computer-based language test. *Language Testing, 20*(3), 295–320.

Clark, J. L. D. (1989). Multipurpose language tests: Is a conceptual and operational synthesis possible? In J.E. Alatis (ed.), *Georgetown University Round Table on Language and Linguistics. Language teaching, testing, and technology: Lessons from the past with a view toward the future* (pp. 206–15). Washington, DC: Georgetown University Press.

Cohen, A. (1998). Strategies and processes in test-taking and SLA. In L. F. Bachman & A. D. Cohen (eds.), *Interfaces between second language acquisition and language testing research* (pp. 90–111). Cambridge: Cambridge University Press.

Cole, N. (1993). Comments on Chapters 1–3. In N. Fredreiksen, R. J. Mislevy & I. I. Bejar (eds.), *Test theory for a new generation of tests* (pp. 72–7). Hillsdale, NJ: Lawrence Erlbaum Associates.

Coniam, D. (1996). Computerized dictation for assessing listening proficiency. *CALICO Journal, 13*(2–3), 73–85.

Coniam, D. (1998). Interactive evaluation of listening comprehension: How the context may help. *Computer-Assisted Language Learning, 11(1),* 35–53.

Coniam, D. (2001). The use of audio or video comprehension as an assessment instrument in the certification of English language teachers: A case study. *System, 29,* 1–14.

Corbel, C. (1993). *Computer-enhanced language assessment.* In G. Brindley (Series ed.) Research Report Series 2. National Centre for English Language Teaching and Research, Marquarie University, Sydney, Australia.

Council of Europe (2001). *Common European Framework of Reference: Learning, teaching, assessment.* Cambridge: Cambridge University Press.

Crookes, G. & Gass, S. M. (eds.) (1993). *Tasks and Language Learning: Integrating theory and practice.* Philadelphia: Multilingual Matters.

Crystal, D. (2001). *Language and the Internet.* Cambridge: Cambridge University Press.

Davidson, F. (1996). *Principles of statistical data handling.* Thousand Oaks, CA: Sage Publications.

DIALANG. (2001) Online: http://dialang.org/info/english/index.htm (Accessed 11 January 2005).

DIALANG Beta Test. (2002). DIALANG Beta Version. Jyväskylä, FI: DIALANG Project, Jyväskylä University.

Discovery School. (2004). *Quiz Center.* DiscoverySchool.com: http://school.dis covery.com/customclassroom/about.html (Accessed 11 January 2005).

Douglas, D. (1998). Testing methods in context-based second language research. In L. F. Bachman & A. D. Cohen (eds.), *Language testing – SLA interfaces* (pp. 141–55). Cambridge: Cambridge University Press.

Douglas, D. (2000). *Assessing languages for specific purposes.* Cambridge: Cambridge University Press.

Dunkel, P. (ed.) (1991). *Computer-assisted language learning and testing: Research issues and practice.* New York: Newbury House.

Dunkel, P. (1999). Research and development of a computer-adaptive test of listening comprehension in the less commonly-taught language Hausa. In M. Chalhoub-Deville (ed.), *Development and research in computer adaptive language testing* (pp. 91–121). Cambridge: University of Cambridge Examinations Syndicate/Cambridge University Press.

Educational Testing Service (1986). *Test of Spoken English.* Princeton, NJ: Educational Testing Service.

Educational Testing Service. (1999). *TOEFL Sampler: An Introduction to Taking the TOEFL Test on Computer.* CD ROM. Princeton, NJ: Educational Testing Service.

Educational Testing Service. (2005a). *Criterion.* Online: http://www.ets.org/criterion/index.html (Accessed 21 September 2005).

Educational Testing Service. (2005b). *Criterion tour.* Online: http://www.ets.org/Media/Products/Criterion/tour2/open.swf (Accessed 21 September 2005).

Embretson, S. (1983). Construct validity: Construct representation versus nomothetic span. *Psychological Bulletin, 93*(1), 179–97.

Embretson, S. (ed.) (1985). Test Design: Developments in psychology and psychometrics. Orlando, FL: Academic Press.

Enlight, A. B. (2004). *TestStation Manager.* Stockholm: http://www. enlight.net/site/ViewPage.action?siteNodeId=226&languageId=1&contentId=-1 (Accessed 11 January 2005).

Fulcher, G. (2000). Computers in language testing. In P. Brett and G. Motteram (eds.), *A special interest in computers* (pp. 93–107). Manchester: IATEFL Publications.

Fulcher. G. (2003). Interface design in computer-based language testing. *Language Testing, 20*(4), 384–408.

GeoHive (2005). GeoHive: Global Statistics. Online: http://www.geohive.com/index.php (Accessed 19 March 2005).

Green, B. F. (1988). Construct validity of computer-based tests. In H. Wainer & H. I. Braun (eds.), *Test validity* (pp. 77–103). Hillsdale, NJ: Lawrence Erlbaum Associates.

Green, B. F., Bock, R. D., Humphreys, L. B., Linn, R. L. & Reckase, M. D. (1984). Technical guidelines for assessing computer adaptive tests. *Journal of Educational Measurement, 21,* 347–60.

Gruba, P. (1997). Exploring digital video material. In R. Debski, J. Gassin & M. Smith (eds.), *Language learning through social computing* (pp. 109–40). Parkville, Vic: Applied Linguistics Association of Australia.

Haas, C. (1996). *Writing technology: Studies on the materiality of literacy.* Mahwah, NJ: Lawrence Erlbaum Associates.

Hagen, L. K. (1994). Constructs and measurement in parameter models of second language acquisition. In E. E. Tarone, S. M. Gass & A. D. Cohen. *Research methodology in second-language acquisition* (pp. 61–87). Hillsdale, NJ: Lawrence Erlbaum Associates.

Half-baked. (2004). Hot Potatoes. Version 6.0.3. Half-baked Software, inc. http://web.uvic.ca/hrd/halfbaked/ (Accessed 11 January 2005).

Halliday, M. A. K. (1994). *An introduction to functional grammar,* 2nd edn. London: Edward Arnold.

Halliday, M. A. K. & Hasan, R. (1989). *Language, context, and text: Aspects of language in a social-semiotic perspective.* Oxford: Oxford University Press.

Hambleton, R. K., Swaminathan, H. & Rogers, H. J. (1991). *Fundamentals of item response theory.* London: Sage Publications.

Hegelheimer, V. & Chapelle, C. A. (2000). Methodological issues in research on learner-computer interactions in CALL. *Language Learning and Technology,* 4(1), 41–59. Online: http://llt.msu.edu/vol4num1/hegchap/default.html

Henning, G. (1987). *A guide to language testing: Development, evaluation, research.* Cambridge, MA: Newbury House.

Henning, G., Anbar, M., Helm, C. & D'Arcy, S. (1993). Computer-assisted testing of reading comprehension: comparisons among multiple-choice and open-ended scoring methods. In D. Douglas & C. A. Chapelle (eds.), *A new decade of language testing research* (pp. 123–31). Alexandria, VA: TESOL Publications.

Higgins, J. J., Lawrie, A. M. & White, A. G. (1999). Recognising coherence: The use of a text game to measure and reinforce awareness of coherence in text. *System, 27,* 339–49.

Hinkel, E. (2003). Simplicity without elegance: Features of sentences in L1 and L2 academic texts. *TESOL Quarterly, 37,* 275–302.

Holland, V. M. (1994). Intelligent tutors for foreign languages: How parsers and lexical semantics can help learners and assess learning. In R. M. Kaplan & J. C. Burstein (eds.), *Proceedings of the Educational Testing Service conference on natural language processing techniques and technology in assessment and education* (pp. 95–108). Princeton, NJ: Educational Testing Service.

Holland, V. M., Kaplan, J. & Sams, M. (eds.) (1994). *Intelligent language tutors: Theory shaping technology* (pp. 153–74). Hillsdale, NJ: Lawrence Erlbaum Associates.

Hughes, A. (1989). *Testing for language teachers.* Cambridge: Cambridge University Press.

IBM Corporation. (2002). *They Also Served: An Album of IBM Special Products,* Vol. 1. Online: http://www-1.ibm.com/ibm/history/exhibits/specialprod1/specialprod1_9.html (Accessed 11 January 2005).

Jamieson, J. & Chapelle, C. A. (1987). Working styles on computers as evidence of second language learning strategies. *Language Learning, 37,* 523–44.

Jamieson, J., Campbell, J., Norfleet, L. & Berbisada, N. (1993). Reliability of a computerized scoring routine for an open-ended task. *System, 21*(3), 305–22.

Jamieson, J., Kirsch, I., Taylor, C. & Eignor, D. (1999). *Designing and evaluating a computer-based TOEFL tutorial.* TOEFL Research Report 62.

Jamieson, J., Taylor, C., Kirsch, I. & Eignor, D. (1998). Design and evaluation of a computer-based TOEFL tutorial. *System, 26,* 485–513.

Kane, M. T. (1992). An argument-based approach to validity. *Psychological Bulletin, 112,* 527–35.

Kane, M. T. (2001). Current concerns in validity theory. *Journal of Educational Measurement, 38,* 319–42.

Kane, M., Crooks, T. & Cohen, A. (1999). Validating measures of performance. *Educational Measurement: Issues and Practice, 18*(2), 5–17.

Kaya-Carton, E., Carton, A. S. & Dandonoli, P. (1991). Developing a computer-adaptive test of French reading proficiency. In P. Dunkel (ed.), *Computer-assisted language learning and testing: Research issues and practice* (pp. 259–84) New York: Newbury House.

Kendrick, M. (1997). Cultural rage and computer literacy: A response to Theodore Roszak. *ALKI: The Washington Library Association Journal 13.2.* Online: http://www.wla.org/alki/jul97/roszak2.html (Accessed 11 January 2005).

Larson, J. W. & Madsen, H. S. (1985). Computer-adaptive language testing: Moving beyond computer-assisted testing. *CALICO Journal, 2*(3), 32–6.

Laurier, M. (1999). The development of an adaptive test for placement in French. In M. Chalhoub-Deville (ed.), *Development and research in computer adaptive language testing* (pp. 122–35). Cambridge: University of Cambridge Examinations Syndicate/Cambridge University Press.

Laurier, M. (2000). Can computerized testing be authentic? *ReCALL, 12*(1), 93–104.

Liskin-Gasparro, J. E. (1984). The ACTFL proficiency guidelines: A historical perspective. In T. V. Higgs (ed.), *Teaching for proficiency: The organizing principle* (pp. 26–28). ACTFL Foreign Language Education Series, 15. Lincolnwood, IL: National Textbook Company.

Longman. (2002). *Business English: Market Leader Interactive.* Online: http://www.longman.com/ae/multimedia/programs/mli.htm# (Accessed 11 January 2005).

Lord, F. M. (1980). *Applications of item response theory to practical testing problems.* Hillsdale. NJ: Lawrence Erlbaum Associates.

Luoma, S. & Tarnanen, M. (2003). Creating a self-rating instrument for second language writing: From idea to implementation. *Language Testing, 20*(4), 440–65.

Madsen, H. S. (1986). Evaluating a computer-adaptive ESL placement test. *CALICO Journal, 4*(2), 41–50.

Madsen, H. S. (1991). Computer-adaptive testing of listening and reading comprehension: The Brigham Young approach. In P. Dunkel (ed.), *Computer-assisted language learning and testing: Research issues and practice* (pp. 237–57). New York: Newbury House.

Malabonga, V., Kenyon, D. & Carpenter, H. (2002). Computer assisted rating: Reliability, efficiency, and perceptions on the COPI. Paper presented at the Language Testing Research Colloquium, Hong Kong, 12–15 December.

Marty, F. (1981). Reflections on the use of computers in second language acquisition. *Studies in Language Learning, 3*(1), 25–53.

McNamara, T. (1996). *Measuring second language performance.* London: Longman.

Messick, S. (1989). Validity. In R. L. Linn (ed.), *Educational Measurement, 3rd edn* (pp. 13–103). NY: Macmillan.

Messick, S. (1994). The interplay of evidence and consequences in the validation of performance assessments. *Educational Researcher, 23*(2), 13–23.

Meunier, L. E. (1994). Computer adaptive language tests (CALT) offer a great potential for functional testing. Yet, why don't they? *CALICO Journal, 11*(4), pp. 23–39.

Mislevy, R. J. (1993). A framework for studying differences between multiple-choice and free-response test items. In R. E. Bennett & W. C. Ward (eds.), *Construction versus choice in cognitive measurement: Issues in constructed response, performance testing, and portfolio assessment* (pp. 75–106). Hillsdale, NJ: Lawrence Erlbaum Associates.

Molholt, G. & Presler, A. M. (1986). Correlation between human and machine ratings of Test of Spoken English passages. In C. W. Stansfield (ed.), *Technology and language testing* (pp. 111–28). Washington DC: Teachers of English to Speakers of Other Languages.

Monaghan, W. & Bridgeman, B. (2005). *E-rater as a quality control on human raters.* R & D Connections, April. Princeton, NJ: Educational Testing Service. Online: http://ftp.ets.org/pub/res/researcher/RD_Connections2. pdf.

Murray, D. (2000). Protean communication: The language of computer-mediated communication. *TESOL Quarterly, 34*(3), 397–421.

Noijons, J. (1994). Testing computer assisted language tests: Towards a checklist for CALT. *CALICO Journal, 12*(1), 37–58.

Norris, J. (in press). Using developmental sequences to estimate English grammar ability: Preliminary design and investigation of a web-based test. *University of Hawaii Working Papers in Applied Linguistics.*

Norris, J. & Ortega, L. (2003). Defining and measuring SLA. In C. J. Doughty & M. H. Long (eds.), *The handbook of second language acquisition* (pp. 718–61). Malden, MA: Blackwell Publishing.

Oller, J. (1979). *Language tests at school.* London: Longman.

Ordinate Corporation. (2002a). Validation summary for PhonePass SET-10. Menlo Park, CA: Author. Online: http://www.ordinate.com (Accessed 11 January 2005).

Ordinate Corporation. (2002b). PhonePass. Online: http://www.ordinate.com (Accessed 11 January 2005).

Otto, S. (1989). Assessment, articulation, accountability: New roles for the language lab. In J. E. Alatis (ed.), *Georgetown University round table on languages and linguistics, 1989. Language teaching, testing, and technology: Lessons from the past with a view toward the future* (pp. 276–87). Washington, DC: Georgetown University Press.

Paltridge, B. (2001). *Genre and the language learning classroom.* Ann Arbor: University of Michigan Press.

Powers, D. E., Burstein, J. C., Chodorow, M., Fowles, M. E. & Kukich, K. (2001*). Stumping E-Rater: Challenging the validity of automated essay scoring. ETS RR 01–03.* Princeton, NJ: Educational Testing Service.

Powers, D. E., Fowles, M. E., Farnum, M. & Ramsey, P. (1994). Will they think less of handwritten essays if others wordprocess theirs? Effects on essay scores of intermingling handwritten and word-processed essays. *Journal of Educational Measurement, 31*(5), 220–33.

Promissor. (2004). *Quality Test Development Services.* Evanston, IL: Promissor, inc. http://www.promissor.com/ (Accessed 11 January 2005).

Purdue University. (2001). *Oral English Proficiency Test.* Version 1.0. West Lafayette, IN: Purdue University.

Questionmark. (2004). *Questionmark Perception.* Questionmark Corporation. http://www.questionmark.com/us/perception/index.htm (Accessed 11 January 2005).

Rassool, N. (1999). *Literacy for sustainable development in the age of information.* Clevedon, UK: Multilingual Matters.

Read, J. (2000). *Assessing vocabulary.* Cambridge: Cambridge University Press.

Reid, J. (1986). Using the Writer's Workbench in composition teaching and testing. In C. Stansfield (ed.), *Technology and language testing* (pp. 167–88). Washington, DC: TESOL Publications.

Respondus. (2004). Version 2.0. Respondus, inc. http://www.respondus.com (Accessed 11 January 2005).

Robinson, P. (2001). Task complexity, cognitive resources, and syllabus design: A triadic framework for examining task influences on SLA. In P. Robinson (ed.), *Cognition and second language instruction* (pp. 287–318). Cambridge: Cambridge University Press.

Roever, C. (2001). Web-based language testing. *Language Learning & Technology, 5*(2), 84–94.

Rost, M. (2003). *Longman English Interactive.* New York: Pearson Education.

Sawaki, Y. (2001). Comparability of conventional and computerized tests of reading in a second language. *Language Learning & Technology, 5*(2), 38–59.

Schaeffer, G. A., Reese, C. M., Steffen, M., McKinley, R. L. & Mills, C. N. (1993). *Field test of a computer-based GRE general test, ETS RR 93–07.* Princeton, NJ: Educational Testing Service.

Singleton, D. & Little, D. (1991). The second language lexicon: some evidence from university-level learners of French and German. *Second Language Research, 7,* 62–81.

Skehan, P. (1998). *A cognitive approach to language learning.* Oxford: Oxford University Press.

Smith, F. (1984). The promise and threat of microcomputers for language learners. In J. Hanscombe, R. Orem & B. Taylor (eds.), *On TESOL '83: The question of control* (pp. 1–18). Washington, DC: Teachers of English to Speakers of Other Languages.

Stansfield, C. (ed.) (1986). *Technology and language testing.* Washington DC: TESOL Publications.

Steinberg, L., Thissen, D. & Wainer, H. (2000). Validity. In H. Wainer, N. J. Dorans, D. Eignor, R. Flaugher, B. F. Green, R. J. Mislevy, L. Steinberg & D. Thissen (2000). *Computer adaptive testing: A primer,* 2nd edn (pp. 185–229). Hillsdale, NJ: Lawrence Erlbaum Associates.

Stevenson, J. & Gross, S. (1991). Use of a computerized adaptive testing model for ESOL/bilingual entry/exit decision making. In P. Dunkel (ed.), *Computer-assisted Language learning and testing: research issues and practice* (pp. 223–36). New York: Newbury House.

Stoynoff, S. & Chapelle, C. A. (2005). *ESOL tests and testing: A resource for teachers and administrators.* Alexandria, VA: TESOL Publications.

Susser, B. (2001). A defense of checklists for courseware evaluation. *ReCALL, 13*(2), 261–76.

Taylor, C., Jamieson, J. & Eignor, D. (2000). Trends in computer use among international students. *TESOL Quarterly, 34(3),* 575–85

Taylor, C., Kirsch, I., Eignor, D. & Jamieson, J. (1999). Examining the relationship between computer familiarity and performance on computer-based language tasks. *Language Learning, 49*(2), 219–74.

Tung, P. (1986) Computer adaptive testing: Implications for language test developers. In C. Stansfield (ed.), *Technology and language testing* (pp. 13–28). Washington, DC: TESOL Publications.

Tyner, K. (1998). *Literacy in a digital world: Teaching and learning in the age of information.* Mahwah, NJ: Lawrence Erlbaum Associates.

University of California, Los Angeles. (2001). WebLAS Web Page: www.humnet. ucla.edu/lasslab/weblas.htm (Accessed 11 January 2005).

University of California, Los Angeles. (2002). WebLAS Demonstration Test. Online: http://www.humnet.ucla.edu/web/departments/alt/weblas_esl_demo/de mo_listen_psych1_vid.htm (Accessed 11 January 2005).

UCLA Applied Linguistics and Center for Digital Humanities. 2001–2003. WebLAS documents. Online: http://www.weblas.ucla.edu/ (Accessed 11 January 2005).

University of Cambridge Local Examination Syndicate. Online: http://www. bulats.org (Accessed 11 January 2005).

University of Surrey. (2001). Online Self-Access Quizzes: http://www.surrey.ac.uk/ ELI/sa/thesis1.html (Accessed 11 January 2005).

Vispoel, W. P. (1998). Psychometric characteristics of computer-adaptive and self-adaptive vocabulary tests: The role of answer feedback and test anxiety. *Journal of Educational Measurement, 35*(2), 155–67.

Vispoel, W. P., Hendrickson, A. B. & Bleiler, T. (2000). Limiting answer review and change on computerized adaptive vocabulary tests: Psychometric and attitudinal results. *Journal of Educational Measurement, 37*(1), 21–38.

Wainer, H. & Braun, H. I. (eds.) (1988). *Test validity.* Hillsdale, NJ: Lawrence Erlbaum Associates.

Wainer, H. & Eignor, D. (2000). Caveats, pitfalls, and unexpected consequences of implementing large-scale computerized testing. In H. Wainer, N. J. Dorans, D. Eignor, R. Flaugher, B. F. Green, R. J. Mislevy, L. Steinberg & D. Thissen (2000). *Computer adaptive testing: A primer,* 2nd edn (pp. 271–99). Hillsdale, NJ: Lawrence Erlbaum Associates.

Wainer, H., Dorans, N. J., Eignor, D., Flaugher, R., Green, B. F., Mislevy, R. J., Steinberg, L. & Thissen, D. (2000). *Computer adaptive testing: A primer,* 2nd edn. Hillsdale, NJ: Lawrence Erlbaum Associates.

Wainer, H., Dorans, N. J., Flaugher, R., Green, B. F., Mislevy, R. J., Steinberg, L. & Thissen, D. (1990). *Computer adaptive testing: A primer.* Hillsdale, NJ: Lawrence Erlbaum Associates.

Wall, D. (1997). Impact and washback in language testing. In C. Clapham and D. Corson (eds.), *Encyclopedia of language and education, vol. VII: Language testing and assessment* (pp. 291–302). Dordrecht, the Netherlands: Kluwer Academic Publishers.

Warschauer, M. (2000). The changing global economy and the future of English teaching. *TESOL Quarterly, 34*(3), 511–35.

Warschauer, M. (1998). Researching technology in TESOL: Determinist, instrumental, and critical approaches. *TESOL Quarterly, 32*(4), 757–61.

Web-based Education Commission. (2000). *The power of the Internet for learning.* Report of the Web-based Education Commission to the President and Congress of the United States. Online: http://www.hpcnet.org/webcommission (Accessed 11 January 2005).

WebCT. (2004). Version 3.0. WebCT, inc. http://www.webct.com (Accessed 11 January 2005).

Weigle, S. C. (2002). *Assessing writing.* Cambridge: Cambridge University Press.

Williamson, D. M., Bejar, I. I. & Hone, A. S. (1999). "Mental model" comparison of automated and human scoring. *Journal of Educational Measurement, 36*(2), 158–84.

Wolfe-Quintero, K., Inagaki, S. & Kim, H-Y. (1998). *Second language development in writing: Measures of fluency, accuracy, and complexity.* Honolulu: University of Hawaii Press.

Wresch, W. (1993). The imminence of grading essays by computer—25 years later. *Computers and Composition, 10*(2), 45–58.

Young, R., Shermis, M. D., Brutten, S. & Perkins, K. (1996). From conventional to computer adaptive testing of ESL reading comprehension. *System, 24*(1), 32–40.

ability *see* communicative competence; language ability

Subject Index

130

Author index